LEATHER PYROGRAPHY

FOX CHAPEL
PUBLISHING
www.FoxChapelPublishing.com

© 2019 by Michele Y. Parsons and Fox Chapel Publishing Company, Inc., 903 Square Street, Mount Joy, PA 17552.

Leather Pyrography is an original work, first published in 2019 by Fox Chapel Publishing Company, Inc. The patterns contained herein are copyrighted by the author. Readers may make copies of these patterns for personal use. The patterns themselves, however, are not to be duplicated for resale or distribution under any circumstances. Any such copying is a violation of copyright law.

ISBN 978-1-4971-0044-2

The Cataloging-in-Publication Data is on file with the Library of Congress.

"Zentangle®," the red square, and "Anything is possible, one stroke at a time" are registered trademarks of Zentangle, Inc. The Zentangle teaching method is patent pending and is used by permission. You'll find wonderful resources, a list of workshops and Certified Zentangle Teachers (CZTs) around the world, a fabulous gallery of inspiring projects, kits, supplies, tiles, pens, and more at *www.zentangle.com*.

To learn more about the other great books from Fox Chapel Publishing, or to find a retailer near you, call toll-free 800-457-9112 or visit us at *www.FoxChapelPublishing.com*.

We are always looking for talented authors. To submit an idea, please send a brief inquiry to acquisitions@foxchapelpublishing.com.

Printed in China
First printing

LEATHER PYROGRAPHY

A Beginner's Guide to Burning Decorative Designs on Leather

Michele Y. Parsons

Fox Chapel
PUBLISHING

CONTENTS

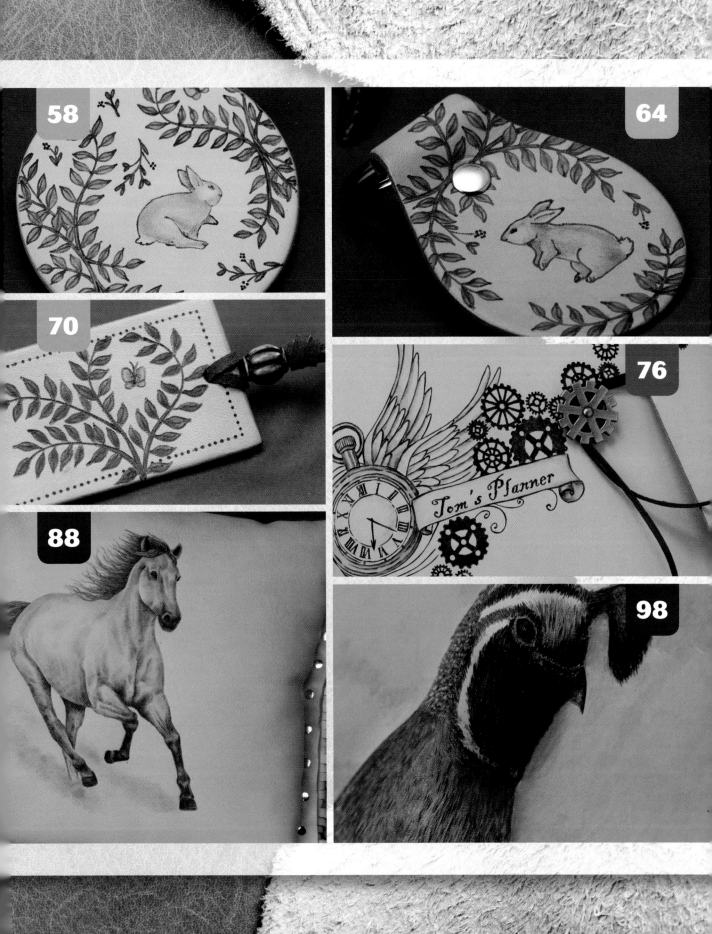

INTRODUCTION

After numerous years as a pyrography artist and instructor, one day I finally tried my hand at leather pyrography and was hooked! Burning on leather is very smooth and relaxing when compared to burning on wood and dealing with wood grain. I embraced leather burning and started teaching small classes as an alternative to woodburning classes while I taught at the International Woodcarving Congress, the Southeastern Woodcarving School, and the Fox Chapel Open House. The reaction I most commonly received from students was that burning on leather is like burning on butter. Students seemed to love the freedom from dealing with wood grain that leather allowed. As I continued the pursuit of leather pyrography, I started selling pyrography-suitable leather products in my online store for my students. Then I began to receive inquiries from customers about leather pyrography, and I realized that I couldn't teach these customers what they needed to know over the phone or through email, especially when they did not have any pyrography experience. That is when I started researching leather pyrography, looking for book or video resources to sell in my online store or to point customers in the direction they needed. However, I found that the information available on leather pyrography is severely lacking—so I decided to write this book.

While deciding what this book would cover, I thought about why leather crafters would want to use pyrography instead of stamping, carving, and modeling leather. I've seen beautiful work done using traditional leathercrafting methods to render images on leather. What pyrography brings to the table is the ability to render extremely fine detail and extremely subtle shading on leather. For example, if a feather was created on leather using traditional tooling methods, the lines would typically be cut. But if I burn the same feather on leather, I can use a thin skew tip and burn thin lines that are so close together that I can render a highly realistic feather. Likewise, I can use a shader pen to portray the subtle tones in an eye's iris to make it appear realistic. Pyrography gives you the ability to create subtleties in your art that other leathercrafts do not.

This book will focus on teaching the basics of pyrography as it applies to leather. I will share with you the methods I use for leather pyrography, but realize there are different methods for accomplishing this art form. After reading this book and trying the techniques and projects, I hope you enjoy leather pyrography as much as I do and continue creating.

Michele Parsons

What's Pyrography?

Why do I use the "fancy" term *pyrography*? The word has its roots in the Greek and Latin words of *pyro* (fire) and *graphy* (writing/drawing). My pyrography students are very familiar with me getting on my soapbox about the use of this special word. Pyrography means burning patterns, text, or images on a variety of mediums, including but not limited to wood, gourds, leather, cork, canvas, tagua nuts, bone, and paper. One of the most popular mediums that people burn is wood. If a person is burning on wood, then woodburning is a perfectly acceptable word to use. Due to the popularity of woodburning, though, I have heard people refer to "woodburning on leather." This is definitely a misnomer, but I've even seen large companies refer to woodburning on leather, too, because they are aware that the public is not familiar with the term pyrography. It would be proper to say leather pyrography is "burning on leather"—just don't use the phrase "woodburning on leather."

Chapter 1

LEATHER

Leather Types and Terms

Leather is a material made from animal skins prepared for use by tanneries. Tanned leather is processed using several methods, such as with chemicals (chrome and dyes) or with natural, organic ingredients (bark and plants), also called vegetable tanning. When leather is burned, fumes are released into the air. Therefore, to avoid breathing chemicals, you do not want to burn on leather that has been chemically processed. **Only burn on undyed, natural vegetable-tanned leather.** Leather at the store or online is not always clearly labeled with the kind of tanning used to produce it. You can identify vegetable-tanned leather (also frequently called veg-tanned leather) by its tan color and its classification as "tooling leather." Vegetable-tanned leather is the type of leather that leathercrafters use for stamping, molding, and tooling. The most common and readily available vegetable-tanned leather in the United States is cowhide.

The smooth side of tanned leather is called the **grain side**. It is the side the hair was on when the animal was alive. The rough side of the processed leather is called the **flesh side**. It is the underside of the hide.

Grain side = Smooth side

Tool and burn leather on this side.

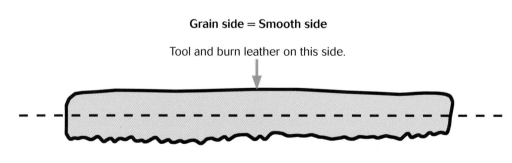

Flesh side = Rough side

Leather Purchasing and Thickness

Whole

Side

Double Shoulder

Single Shoulder

Back

Belly

Leather is cut and marked in square feet (square meters) by the tannery to be sold as a whole hide or commonly cut parts of the hide:

- Whole: the entire animal skin or hide
- Side: half of the entire animal skin or hide from the neck to the tail
- Double Shoulder: the shoulder area from a Whole
- Single Shoulder: the shoulder area from a Side
- Back: the portion of a Side with the Belly removed
- Belly: the portion of a Side with the Back removed

Leather is priced by the quality of the grain (smooth) side. If there are a lot of blemishes, such as cuts or branding marks, the hide is sold as Economy leather. If there are only a few blemishes, the hide is sold as Good Quality leather. Finally, if the hide is blemish free, it is classified as Excellent Quality leather.

Leather is also priced by the weight of a square foot (square meter) of the hide. When leather is processed, it is split so that its thickness becomes more even. Due to natural variation in thickness even after splitting the hide, leather is marked and sold using a weight range, such as 6 to 7 oz. Due to the weight being determined by the thickness of the leather, there are common usages of leather in certain weight ranges (see table on page 10). Leather of any thickness can be used for pyrography. However, care must be taken on the thinnest leathers with the skew pen tips. The skew is like a knife and, when hot, can slice right through the leather if pressure is applied.

A simple gauge can help in readily identifying the thickness of leather.

Thickness	Thickness in Ounces	Thickness in Inches	Thickness in Millimeters	Characteristics	Common Uses
───	2 to 3 oz	¹⁄₃₂" to ³⁄₆₄"	0.8mm to 1.2mm	very thin and pliable	Used for molding, embossing, quilting, appliqués, linings, and jewelry
───	3 to 4 oz	³⁄₆₄" to ¹⁄₁₆"	1.2mm to 1.6mm	thin and pliable	Used for molding, embossing, repoussé, appliqués, linings, thin clutches, thin wallets, and billfolds
───	4 to 5 oz	¹⁄₁₆" to ⁵⁄₆₄"	1.6mm to 2.0mm	thin and pliable	Used for molded leather masks, appliqués, clutches, wallets, billfolds, wristbands, and conceal carry holsters
───	5 to 6 oz	⁵⁄₆₄" to ³⁄₃₂"	2.0mm to 2.4mm	sturdy and pliable	Used for die stamping, small cases, and notebook and journal covers
───	6 to 7 oz	³⁄₃₂" to ⁷⁄₆₄"	2.4mm to 2.8mm	sturdy and flexible	Used for die stamping, handbags, medium cases, journal covers, and straps
───	7 to 8 oz	⁷⁄₆₄" to ¹⁄₈"	2.8mm to 3.2mm	sturdy	Used for die stamping, knife sheaths, narrow belts, straps, handles, and small holsters
───	8 to 9 oz	¹⁄₈" to ⁹⁄₆₄"	3.2mm to 3.6mm	very sturdy	Used for die stamping, belts, holsters, and saddle bags
───	9 to 10 oz	⁹⁄₆₄" to ⁵⁄₃₂"	3.6mm to 4.0mm	extremely sturdy	Used for die stamping, belts wider than 1½" (3.8cm), and larger holsters

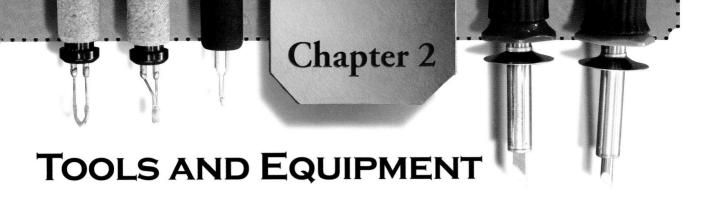

Chapter 2

Tools and Equipment

A leather pyrography studio can be very simple and set up in a small area. Here is a detailed list of the various equipment and tools that you will need.

Workspace Equipment

Tables and Chairs

Pyrography can be accomplished holding a piece of art while sitting in a chair, on a couch, or sitting at a table. It is important to have your arm and shoulder at a comfortable height while burning. When your burning surface is too high, it forces your shoulder to be raised, which will create tension in your shoulder and neck after extended periods of time, and which also reduces the amount of control you have with your pen. Working on a table is ideal because it provides room for your burning equipment and tools and, with the proper chair height, provides an ideal shoulder height for the best control when burning. However, I have found that there are times when working on a large object, such as a box or bowl, that working on a table would make the burning surface too high, so working in a chair or on a couch becomes necessary. When working in a chair or on a couch, you will need to provide a steady surface to hold your equipment. A supplemental table, a large tray, or a large wood board can provide space for your equipment. Ensure that it is stable so the equipment cannot be knocked over and hot pens cannot roll off.

Fans

A carbon-activated filter fan.

Using fans can help reduce the amount of burning fumes that reach your lungs and help with the smell of burning leather. There are several fan options to choose from.

You can use a **small fan** to blow the fumes away from your work. Do not blow the fan toward your work, because the moving air will change the temperature of your pen tips as you move in and out of the airflow.

You need to have good ventilation in the room, such as open doors and windows; otherwise, the fan will just circulate the fumes around the room and you will still inhale them.

Another option is to use a **carbon-activated filter fan**. Activated carbon traps fume particles. These fans will not clean the air one hundred percent, but the difference is obvious: A room that uses a carbon-activated filter fan only has a faint odor that can barely be detected when compared to a room that is using a regular fan for ventilation. Carbon-activated filter fans only work well when the fan is right next to the burning material. The fumes have to go through the fan immediately when burning; otherwise, they will simply escape and circulate around the room anyway. I set my fan very close to my work and, because I use a rotating easel, I place my fan on a couple of wood blocks to raise it high enough to trap the fumes as they roll off the edge of the artwork. I recommend carbon-activated fans that have an airflow rated at least 85 cfm (cubic feet per minute) (or 2.5 cubic meters per minute) to remove the smoke. There are some inexpensive models on the market, but they don't have enough fan power to make a difference.

Another option is to build a **ventilation system** that vents directly to the outdoors. This is a permanent option that does not allow for carrying your work to a temporary location, such as when you can take a fan to a pyrography class. A ventilation system can include several options: a hooded vent located over the burning area, a fan to blow the fumes outdoors, or a carbon-activated filter fan to draw the fumes through the filter before they are channeled outdoors.

Easels

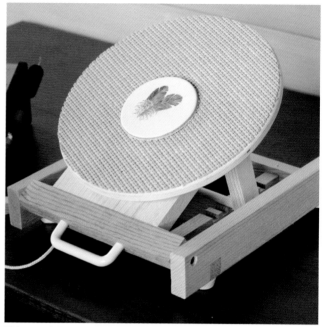

This easel tilts and rotates.

Tilting and rotating easels are considered optional equipment for pyrography, but they offer several advantages.

As we grow older and our eyes don't see as well, or if we simply don't have great eyesight to begin with, there is a natural tendency to lean in over our work and put our face close to the action so we can see better. Doing this means the burning fumes go straight up into our nose and eyes. Using a **tilted easel** or a **slant board** allows you to sit upright in your chair while bringing the surface of the artwork closer to your face so you can see better. The fumes still rise vertically from the surface, but your face is not directly over those fumes. The tilted table or slant board also reduces overhead lighting from reflecting off your burning at an angle that causes glare. Additionally, a tilted table or slant board allows burning at the top of a large piece while sitting, as opposed to having to lay the large work on a flat table and then lean far over it to burn for sometimes hours, which can strain your back. Because of the slant of a tilted easel, it is helpful to cover the surface in non-slip shelving liner to prevent the artwork from sliding.

A **rotating table** provides the benefit of being able to quickly turn your work without delaying or stopping burning to turn your artwork. The ability to turn your piece while burning is very important for stroke direction so that you are not forcing your hand and arm into uncomfortable positions, following curves in a continuous motion while using skew tips, and creating directional shading fades.

Lighting

Do not underestimate the importance of good lighting. The better you can see your work, the better you will burn. If the room you are working in has low lighting, even if it is only at night or on overcast days, supplement the lighting with a portable lamp.

Pyrography Burners

There are two types of pyrography burners: those that heat solid brass tips (solid point burners) and those that heat nichrome wire tips (wire tip burners). Both types of burners have several options, advantages, and disadvantages.

Solid Point Burners

Solid point burners, sometimes called craft burners, look similar to soldering guns. The name solid point refers to the solid brass tips, which come in a variety of shapes. The tips are interchangeable and screw into the handles. A solid point burner can be purchased as either a single temperature burner or a burner with a rheostat (a current regulator) to adjust the temperature.

Advantages of solid point burners include:

- The cost to purchase the burner and tips is very inexpensive.

- The unit and tips are very portable.

- The brass tips hold heat very well and, therefore, burn dark blacks very well.

Disadvantages of solid point burners include:

- Brass is very malleable when heated, which means it gets very soft and can bend easily when pressure is put on the tips. It also means the threads that screw the tip into the handle can easily be stripped if the tip is hot while taking it in or out of the handle.

- Solid point burner handles get very hot, especially the handles that are only plastic with no rubber cover.

- The solid point burner handle is very large in diameter and the hand position is a long way from the point of the tip; both of these features reduce the amount of control you have over your strokes.

- Brass tips take a long time to heat up and cool down; depending on the tip, it may take as long as five minutes. This makes changing tips very time-consuming.

- Brass tips are limited in selection and do not have the ability to produce the extremely detailed markings that nichrome wire tips can produce.

- Solid point burners that do not have a rheostat can only burn at one temperature: very hot. In order to burn light markings, you have to burn quickly or burn while the pen is heating up or cooling down.

Leather burns at a lower temperature than wood, so companies such as Walnut Hollow® and Tandy® Leather have manufactured solid point burners that burn at a lower temperature, such as 675°F (355°C), specifically for leather. The issues regarding a large diameter handle, distance to the point, and inability to easily control light versus darker burning still exist for these special leather solid point burners.

Wire Tip Burners

Wire tip burners, also called nichrome wire burners or variable-temperature burners, consist of a transformer/control box connected to an electric pen by a cord. The burners can be purchased as either single-pen units or dual (two)-pen units. If you purchase a dual-pen unit, you cannot use both pens at the same time. You use a switch to toggle back and forth between the pens, which allows you to have two pens ready to go at any time. The ability to have two pens ready to burn saves wear and tear on the pens by reducing the plugging and unplugging. A dual-pen unit also allows options for configuring different cords. For example, you can have both a standard and heavy-duty weight cord plugged into your control box. Standard weight cords are used for general burning, and heavy-duty weight cords are used for high temperature burning, such as dark shading or burning on materials that need higher heat (like bone). A dual-pen unit can also be configured with different cords so that multiple brand pens can be used on the same unit, such as a cord that accepts Razertip® pens and a cord that accepts Colwood and Optima pens.

Advantages of wire tip burners include:

- The nichrome wire pens are extremely sensitive and can usually heat up and cool down within seconds. This gives you the ability to rapidly change from really dark burning to really light burning and also allows pen tips to be changed quickly.

- The pen handles are much cooler than on solid point burners.

- The pens are very similar to writing pens, having a thinner grip and designed so your holding hand is near the tip. This allows the hand to be close to the surface of the material, which means you can easily rest your hand on the material, giving you more support and control.

- Nichrome wire pen tips come in a large variety of shapes and sizes.

- Nichrome wire pen tips can be extremely small and thin, allowing for very detailed renderings.

Disadvantages of wire tip burners include:

- Wire tip burners and their accessories cost more than solid point burners.
- Nichrome wire shader pens lose their heat rapidly when they come in contact with material surface. To compensate for this rapid heat loss, shorter pen strokes when shading are required to maintain the heat level.

Pens and Pen Tips

Pyrography pens come in two styles: fixed tip and replaceable tip. Regardless of style, the tips themselves come in different categories: writer, skew, shader, and branding/specialty.

Fixed Tip Pens

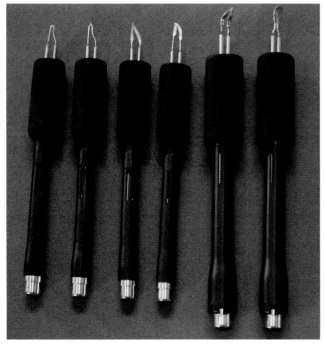

A fixed tip pen refers to a pen that has its tip permanently soldered to the pen handle, providing what is considered by most pyrographers to be the best connection possible. Most manufacturers of wire tip burners sell fixed tip pens for their units at an approximate cost of $20 to $32 per pen. The entire pen is connected and disconnected from the burner's cord.

Replaceable Tip Pens

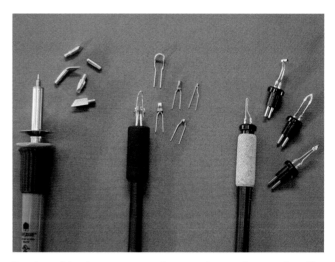

Replaceable tip pens come in two pieces: the pen handle and the tip. The advantage of purchasing replaceable tip pens is that once you buy the handle, you only need to buy the tip, which is very inexpensive compared to purchasing a fixed tip pen. The cost of individual wire tips can range from $5 to $17, depending on the manufacturer and the type of tip.

There are a few ways replaceable tip wires connect to their pen handles. On solid point burners, the tip is screwed into the handle. On some wire tip burners, the replaceable tips are soldered into a bushing to create a replaceable component. This component is pushed into the handle to complete the pen. In order to take the replaceable component out of the handle, a tip puller must be used. Other manufacturers sell the tips as wires that are attached to the handle with screws. Sometimes these wire tips are thickened at the ends and slip into channels in the handle before the screws are tightened. Other times the wire tips are the same size on the ends and are simply held in place between the screw and handle tip holder and then tightened. This screw method allows for purchasing nichrome wire and making your own tips.

Pen Tip Categories

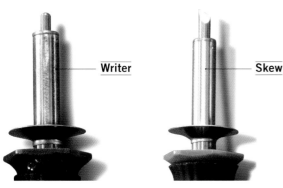

Writer Skew

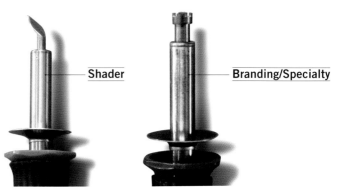

Shader Branding/Specialty

When counting the number of pen varieties available, manufacturers count both their fixed tip pens and replaceable tip pens even though the tips themselves may be the same. Razertip Industries has the largest selection, with over 900 varieties available! This can seem overwhelming to new pyrographers. To make it easier, understand that all pens are grouped into one of four categories by their usage: **writer**, **skew**, **shader**, or **branding/specialty**. Although any pen can be used in a variety of ways, its category designation is based on its designed primary function.

Writer Category

All pens and tips in the writer category have the same characteristic: the end of the tip that touches the material is rounded. It can either be a bent wire, a rounded endpoint, or a rounded ball. This rounded edge allows the tip to glide over the surface of the material and not get caught in grain or texture. This also allows the user to freely draw circles and loops such as in writing, hence the name of this category.

Characteristics of writer pens:

- The edge of the tip is rounded (bent wire, rounded endpoint, or ball), which allows the tip to glide over the surface of the material and easily make circles and loops.

- The burned markings from a writer tip have soft edges.

- The burned markings from a writer tip are on the surface and produce a shade of light to dark brown on leather.

Skew Category

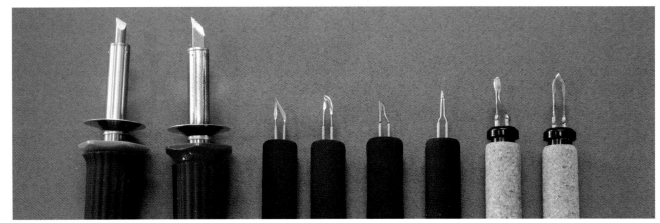

The skew category encompasses pens and tips that have a knife edge. The skew tips cut the surface of the material while it is burning. Since the skew is cutting the material,

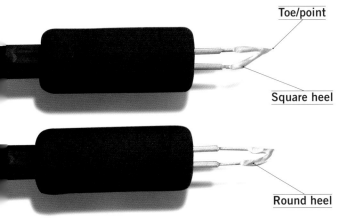

Toe/point

Square heel

Round heel

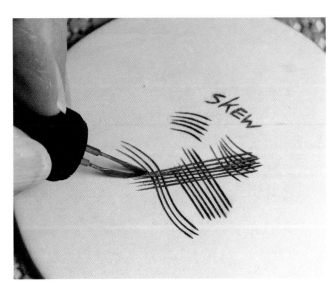

it is riding below the surface of the material and cannot move sideways to make a circle in one motion. If you try to make a circle while the tip is in the material, the tip will either skip out of the material or break when you try to move it sideways. Therefore, skews can only make straight lines or curved lines. The only way to make a circle using a skew is to draw the circle using tiny connected segments.

A skew tip is named for the tilted, skewed angle of the knife tip. The tip consists of a point (or toe) and a heel. The point can be pointed or rounded. The heel (lower angle from the point) can be squared or rounded. A square heel is primarily designed to make perfectly straight lines when the heel is lowered into the surface material, thus creating a self-tracking line. You can make a curved line with a square-heeled skew if you lift the heel out of the material. A round-heeled skew is primarily designed to make curved lines.

Characteristics of skew pens:

- The edge of the skew tip is a knife that cuts the material as it is burning.

- The skew tip rides below the surface of the material, which prevents the making of a circle or loop in one motion.

- Lines made with a skew tip are very sharp.

- A skew tip makes very dark, almost black lines on leather.

Shader Category

Shader tips are very similar to skew tips in that they also have knife edges. The difference is that most shader tips are bent at an approximate 45° angle. This allows the tip to be placed on the surface of the material similarly to a clothing iron. There are a large variety of shader tips available— extra small to extra large, pointed toe or rounded toe, spoon shaped (the edges are rolled up to form a spoon) and closed/solid "iron" shaped or open shaped. The primary purpose of a shader is to create varying tones on the material similar to the result of using a paintbrush.

Characteristics of shader pens:

• The edge of a shader tip has a knife edge similar to a skew. However, the shader tip is usually bent so that the tip rides on the surface of the material.

• The shader tip burns flat tones from light to dark.

Branding/Specialty Category

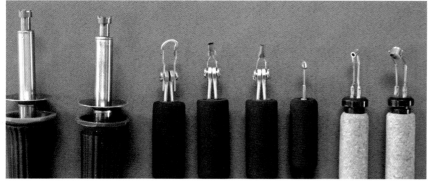
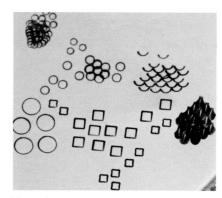

Pen tips that are not in the writer, skew, or shader category fall in the branding/specialty category. Examples of these pen tips are circles, squares, and a variety of shapes that are all pressed onto the material and held until the shape is burned, much like a cattle brander. Feather formers are also in this category. To use a feather former, the tip is pressed onto the material and then dragged to create the illusion of feather barbs. There are also other specialty tips, such as wax application tips used for writing or drawing with beeswax to decorate eggs (such as Ukrainian Easter eggs).

Characteristics of branding/specialty pens:

• The shaped tips of branders are pressed onto the material and held until the shape is burned (branded) into the material.

• Feather forming tips are pressed and then dragged to form feather barbs.

Cords and Adapters

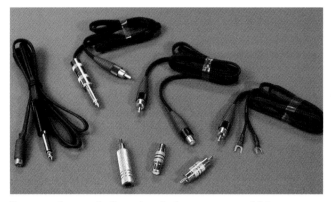

Pyrography cords for wire tip burners are sold in different weights, typically 18 gauge and 16 gauge. Standard weight cords use an 18-gauge wire for maximum flexibility and sometimes are referred to as super-flex or ultra-flex cords. Heavy-duty weight cords use a 16-gauge wire to allow the maximum current flow. Heavy-duty cords are not as flexible as standard cords, but they supply more current for hotter burning, such as when shading and branding.

Pyrography cords can be wired directly into the burner, or they can have a unique connection for the type of burner they are attaching to, such as lug endings for a screw connection, phone jack plugs, or RCA plugs. The end of the cord that attaches to the pen will have either a male or female RCA connection, depending on what brand pen you are using. For example, if you have a Colwood burner, your cord will have two lugs that connect to the screws on the back of the burner. The other end of the cord will have a female RCA plug that connects to the end of the Colwood pens. If you want to use a Razertip pen on a Colwood burner, you would need to use an adapter to switch the orientation of the cord, because the Razertip pen needs a male RCA plug. This switch in orientation can be accomplished by using either an adapter cord or an adapter connector.

Adapter connectors are inexpensive and look similar to an audio connector. However, you should avoid using audio connectors, because they are not designed to support the high current needed for burning. Only use high-current connectors. Adapter connectors do add a little extra weight onto the end of your pen. For this

reason, some pyrographers prefer to purchase an adapter cord that will connect to their burner so they can use another brand pen.

Note: Some burners use more electric current than other brands, so some brands do not intermix well. Razertip burners output very little current, so their pens are designed to respond quickly using little current. I've had no issue connecting Razertip pens on Colwood or Optima burners, but I did have problems when connecting Razertip pens to a Burnmaster® burner. Because Burnmaster burners output a lot of current, the temperature could not be turned much higher than a 1 on the dial without the Razertip pens glowing red.

Pyrography Torches

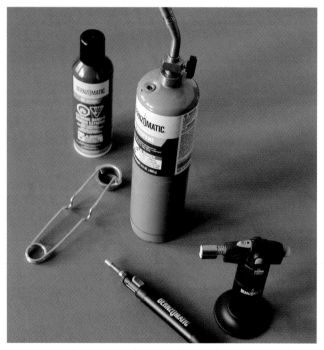

Propane or butane torches can be used in pyrography to rapidly darken areas or to achieve a burned, "airbrushed" effect. Typically, smaller butane micro torches or butane pencil torches are used because they can be controlled to burn in smaller areas. These torches can be purchased at hardware or home improvement stores. Use these torches in a ventilated area away from flammable materials and have a fire extinguisher handy.

Additional Accessories

There are a lot of pyrography accessories that are very handy to have in your studio. Following is a tour through a variety of additional tools and materials available to you. They're all optional; try out the ones that interest you.

Magnifying Glasses

Magnifying glasses are very useful when burning so that you can see the image you are burning better. There are a variety of magnifying glass options that are available: a magnifying glass (with or without lighting) that clips or clamps to your table, magnifying glasses that attach to your own glasses, or magnifying visors that sit on your head.

Cutting and Pounding Boards (Cutting/Tooling/ Gripper Mats and Slabs)

Left to right (clockwise): Poundo board, granite slab, self-healing cutting mat, cutting mat, non-slip mat.

Mats that are designed to protect your work surface while you are cutting and tooling on your leather also cut down on the noise. There are specialty mats for cutting that self-heal where the cut was made so that the surface remains flat. Poundo boards are designed to withstand the crushing blows from punching leather for sewing, making stud and buckle holes, and applying rivets. Poundo boards are about ³⁄₁₆" to ½" (0.5 to 1.3cm) thick boards that also dampen the sound of stamping leather when placed under stone slabs. Stone slabs (marble, granite, or quartz) are useful to resist the mallet blow when stamping leather, giving a clean, even impression. Stone slabs are a little over 1" to 2½" (2.5 to 6.4cm) thick to withstand the impact. Gripper mats are non-slip mats made from non-slip shelving liner. These mats are handy to hold the leather during a dry pattern transfer so the pattern can be taped to the table and not to the leather.

Transfer Paper (Unwaxed)

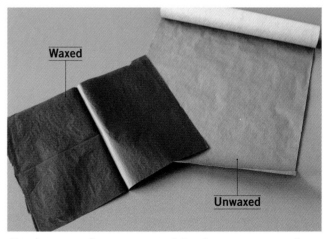

Waxed

Unwaxed

Graphite transfer paper is used for dry pattern transfer. Use unwaxed transfer paper so the graphite will erase when you are through burning—waxed transfer paper does not erase as easily on leather. Waxed transfer paper looks extremely black, whereas unwaxed transfer paper looks gray. **Do not use carbon paper** (used for old typewriter duplication), because the carbon will fuse to the leather once it is heated and cannot be erased.

Office Supplies (Pens, Rulers, Tape, Scissors, Erasers, Razor Blades)

Standard office supplies, such as rulers and tape, should be on hand to be used as needed. Using a red pen for dry pattern transfer will help you see where you have traced the pattern. White rubber erasers and kneaded erasers work well to remove graphite from the leather after pattern transfers. Razor blades can be used to remove excess buildup on your flat tips and can be used for minor burning touchups on leather.

Leathercrafting Tools (Stamps, Punches, Burnishers, Modeling Tools, Riveters, Cutting Tools, Hardware)

Depending on the leather projects you create and the leathercrafting techniques you want to incorporate into your projects, you may want leather stamps, punches, burnishers, modeling tools, cutting tools, sewing tools, rivets, snaps, conchos, or other hardware.

Leathercrafting Materials (Leather, Lace, Leather Kits)

Depending on your projects, you may want additional leather hides, leather cutouts, leather kits, or leather lace.

Leather Finishing Products (Glues, Color, Finishes)

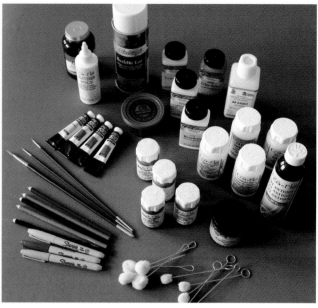

Depending on how you want to color and finish your projects, you may want leather glues, dyes, markers, paints, stains, daubers, brushes, and finishes.

Heat and Grime Protection (Gloves/Finger Guards)

Left to right (clockwise): Cotton glove, silicon finger guards, leather glove, SmudgeGuard™.

The majority of pyrography pen handles are designed to reduce the heat on your hand, but if the heat is bothering your hand, there are options available, such as using a leather glove, self-sticking finger tape, or silicon finger guards. Using a specialty glove called a SmudgeGuard or a cotton glove will protect your leather from your hand oils and sweat.

Cleaning and Polishing Tools

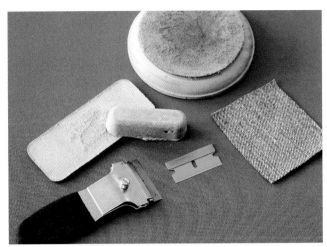

Left to right (clockwise from lower left): Razor blade with handle, leather polishing strop, jeweler's rouge, leather polishing disk, denim cleaning cloth, razor blade.

To achieve the best burning possible, you will need supplies to keep your pen tips cleaned and polished. See page 24 for details on cleaning and polishing your pen tips.

Carrying Cases and Pen Protection

If you transport your pyrography equipment to classes or club meetings, you'll want a case to protect and hold your equipment. Whether you use a specially designed case, a tool bag, or a box, ensure that your burner has its cords protected from being cut or damaged. Protect your pen tips from damage, too; do not place them loosely in a box or the case. Instead, use the manufacturer's storage tubes they were sold in, a tool roll for pens/gouges, or an artist's paintbrush case.

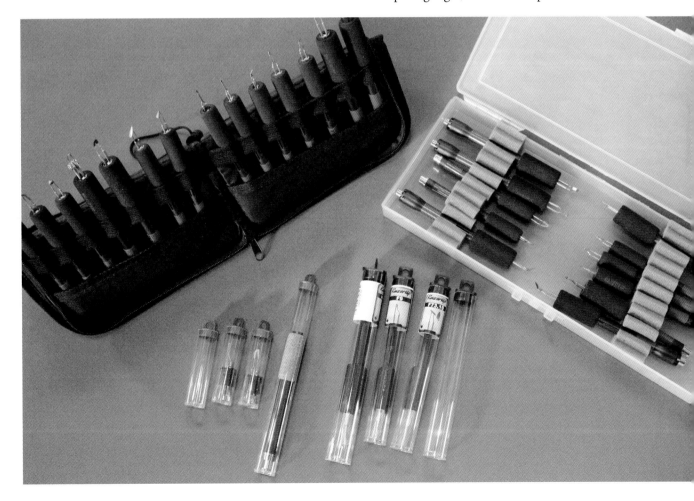

Chapter 3

TECHNIQUES

Setting Up to Burn

Equipment Setup

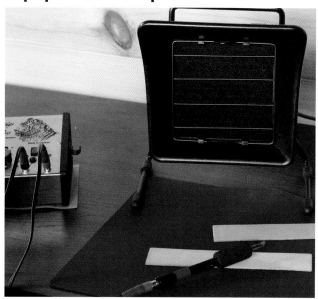

After deciding where you will be burning, set up your burner, pens, lighting, fan, easel, and accessories on a stable surface. (See page 11 for the chapter detailing all these tools.) Place your burner and electrical connections on the side of your dominant hand (if you are left-handed, place your tools on your left side; if right-handed, place them on your right side). This positioning stops your cords from crossing your artwork. Place the fan blowing away from your work, or, if you have a carbon-activated filter fan, place it very close to your work so the smoke goes through the fan. Open the doors and windows if possible for additional ventilation. Inspect the pen tips you will be using to ensure they are cleaned, polished, and ready for burning.

Cleaning and Polishing Pen Tips

Burning causes carbon to build up on your pens, which in turn causes uneven burning or carbon smudges that do not erase. To achieve the best burning from your pens, you will need to clean and polish your pens.

Cleaning on denim.

Cleaning is a continuous process to keep excess debris and carbon off the tip of the pen. I recommend wiping your pen tips on a piece of denim fabric while you work, especially if you see any black specks (carbon dust) when you are burning. You can wipe the pen tip on the denim while the pen is hot, but the heat will pass through the denim onto your table or project. For this reason, I recommend placing your denim on a scrap piece of wood or heat-resistant silicone mat.

Polishing on a leather strop.

Polishing is a process that you should do less often so you do not round the edges of your tip with the abrasive over time. I polish my tips when the cleaning process stops getting results (seeing carbon dust quickly after you just wiped it on the denim) or when I feel the tip dragging across the surface of the leather. Polishing is done with a leather strop, which is a piece of thick leather (flesh side up) or a thinner piece of leather attached to a piece of wood for stability. A honing compound, such as aluminum oxide or jeweler's rouge (red or blue), is rubbed on the strop. Once the strop is charged with the honing compound, rub the tip on the compound until you achieve a polished surface. Then wipe the tip on a cloth to remove the compound before you heat the tip. Polishing is done with your burner turned off so that you are not heating the compound and breathing its fumes. For the beveled knife edge on the skews, lean the tip to one side and run the beveled edge on the compound several times. Then lean the tip to the other side and polish the remaining beveled edge. For writing tips, lean the tip in multiple directions to polish all sides of the rounded tip surface.

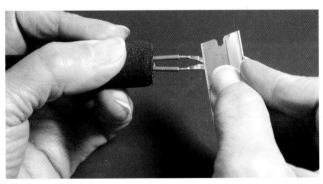
Removing debris.

If you get a **large amount of debris** stuck to the tip of your pen, you can remove the excess debris by taking a single-edge razor blade and scraping the debris off the tip. The excess debris buildup is common on the shader tips because they have such a large amount of metal on the leather. Hold the razor blade flat and parallel to the tip surface and gently scrape without letting the razor blade corners scratch the tip.

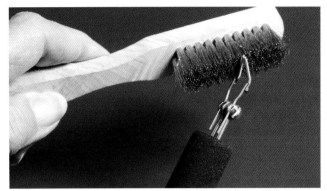
Cleaning with a brush.

Another method of cleaning pen tips, especially ones that are odd shaped or textured, such as feather formers or keeled snake scales, is to use a **soft brass wire brush**. The brush has to be very soft so it does not leave scratches on the tip. Do not use a brass brush commonly purchased at a hardware or home improvement store. These coarse brushes are designed to remove rust off metal and will leave scratch marks on your tip.

Do not clean with sandpaper!

Even though it is a popular method, I **do not recommend cleaning pen tips with sandpaper** or sandpaper pads. Think about it this way: Imagine a ball writer tip that is perfectly round. Then imagine rubbing the ball tip on sandpaper over and over. Sandpaper, whether common or fine grit, is abrasive enough to remove metal from your tips. A perfectly smooth, round ball will end up becoming a faceted ball over time. For this reason, I only use sandpaper when I actually want to reshape a tip.

Leather Preparation

Leather Care

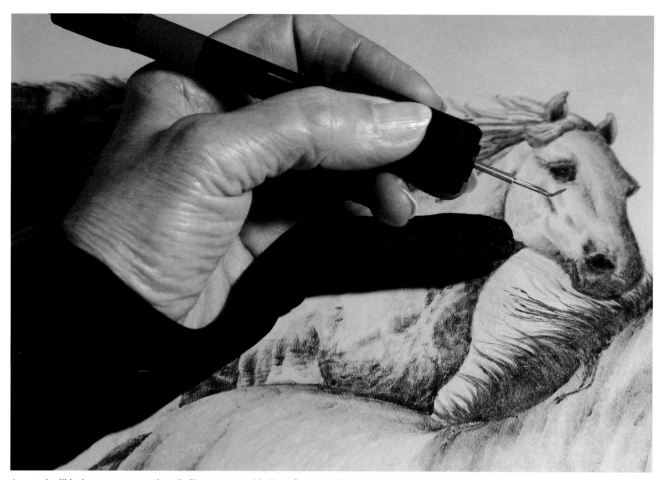

A guard will help prevent your hand oils, sweat, and lotions from getting on your work.

Before leather has a finishing product applied, it is susceptible to damage from water spots, hand oils, sweat, lotions, and sun damage. Although leathercrafters wet leather to prepare it for tooling and carving, they wet the entire surface so it dries evenly. If you manage to gets spots of water on the leather, they will show unless you wet the entire surface, meaning you will have to wait until the leather dries completely before you can burn it. Avoid getting your hand oils, sweat, or lotion on the leather by wearing a cotton glove or a SmudgeGuard (a specialty glove designed to protect the surface while only covering part of your hand for temperature and breathability comfort). Alternatively, place a clean, dry cloth or paper on your working surface to rest your hand.

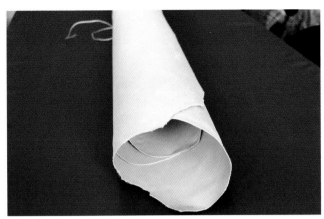

Roll leather grain side in to store it.

Sun will darken vegetable-tanned leather, so if you have only part of the leather exposed to the sun, you will have two-toned leather. Therefore, protect your leather until you are ready to use it in your projects by rolling large pieces with the grain side inward and tying it with a string, storing your leather in a dark room, or wrapping your leather in paper to keep it out of the sunlight.

Stabilizing Leather

When tool stamping and texturing the surface of leather, thin leather can stretch and move, causing the leather to distort its shape and curl. To prevent this from happening, you can glue thinner leather (4 to 6 oz.) to a backing to stabilize the leather. The backing needs to be stiff enough to combat any warping. Common backing materials include heavy chipboard, heavy cardstock, or mat board. Spread rubber cement on the backing only and then firmly attach the leather.

Pattern Transfer

You can use a soft graphite pencil (2B to 9B) to draw a pattern directly on the leather, or you can transfer your pattern onto the leather using either a wet or dry transfer technique.

Wet Transfer

Leathercrafters typically transfer a pattern by applying water to the leather using a sponge or sprayer on the grain side. Once wet, the water is allowed to absorb into the leather, making it pliable. Then the pattern is either scribed onto the damp leather using a stylus (metal ball tip on the end of a handle that looks like a pen), or, if using a Craftaid® pattern (pattern embossed on plastic), the pattern is pressed into the damp leather using a brayer (roller). If you are using a wet transfer method, the leather has to completely dry before burning on it.

Dry Transfer

I use the same dry transfer method I use on wood to transfer a pattern onto leather so that I don't have to wait for the leather to dry before burning the image.

1. Place the completely dry leather on a hard, flat surface. I like to place my smaller leather pieces on non-slip shelving liner that is taped to the table so my pieces do not move.

2. Position the pattern over the leather and tape the pattern to the table. If you prefer to tape your pattern to the leather, test your tape on a scrap piece of the same leather. I have found that most tapes leave whitish marks on the leather when

removed. There are some exceptions, like low-tack green painter's tape, but test before using your tape on leather.

3. When taping your pattern, place two pieces of tape with a gap in between on one side of the pattern (or you can use a long piece of tape) to ensure the pattern does not misalign after being lifted and lowered while tracing.

4. Slip a piece of unwaxed transfer/graphite paper under the pattern with the transfer/graphite side down next to the leather. (Do not use waxed graphite paper or carbon paper; see page 20.)

5. Trace a few lines of the pattern with a pen or pencil, and then lift your pattern and transfer paper to check whether you are successfully transferring onto the leather. Also check that the transferred lines are dark enough to see but not so dark that you'll have trouble erasing them when you are done with your project.

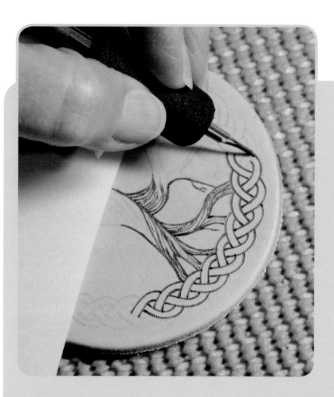

Tip:

After your pattern has been transferred with transfer/graphite paper, avoid smearing and erasing the graphite while burning. You can achieve this by starting your burn on the side closest to your dominant hand and working your way across the picture so that your hand is crossing only areas that are already burned. Alternatively, you can place paper on the transferred lines and avoid too much hand movement on any particular location until that area has been burned.

Tip:

Using a red or colored pen when transferring your pattern will allow you to easily see which lines you have already traced over.

Burning Techniques

When learning how to burn leather, it is easier to learn the techniques on flat, two-dimensional leather before adding the complexity of working on a modeled, three-dimensional surface. There are several techniques that are similar no matter which pen tip is being used, as well as techniques specific to certain pen tips. It's all covered in this section, so learn before you burn.

Pen Temperature

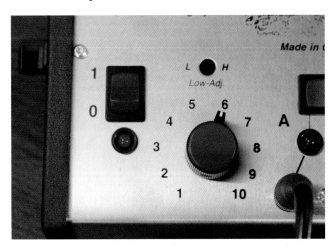

Wire tip pyrography burners have a temperature dial to adjust the heat, allowing you to control the burn of lines and marks from light to dark. The temperature setting on a wire tip machine should generally fall between the 10 and 2 o'clock positions on the dial (usually 3.5 to 7.5 on your dial) for most of your burning. Avoid setting the temperature so high that the wire pen tip starts glowing bright red like a hot poker. It is okay for the tip to have a faint red glow when burning high temperatures on materials such as bone. However, allowing the pen tip to glow bright, fluorescent red anneals the tip metal, leaving the thin wire tip brittle when it cools and making it susceptible to breakage.

Avoid turning the temperature dial up too high and then burning really fast. This will result in your fingers feeling hot from the high heat and also causes a tendency to produce blobs from any hesitation.

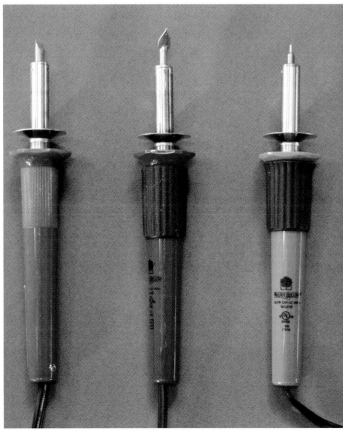

The green pen is rated at 950°F (510°C)—too hot for leather. The red pen is a variable temperature pen and can be used on low setting for leather. The tan pen is rated at 675°F (355°C), perfect for use on leather.

When using a solid point burner with one heat setting, the only ways to control making light and dark lines is to either adjust the speed of the burning pen or to burn lighter lines and marks while the burner is heating up or cooling down. Since leather burns faster than wood, a one-temperature, solid point burner made specifically for leather is easier to control than a general-purpose solid point burner because the leather burner's maximum temperature is lower. For example, a general-purpose solid point burner can have a temperature of 950°F (510°C), whereas a leather solid point burner can have a temperature of 675°F (355°C).

Pen Speed

The lighter lines were burned quickly; the darker lines were burned slowly.

The speed at which the pen is moved affects the color and consistency of a burned line or mark. The faster the pen is moved, the lighter the line will be, because there was not enough time in contact with the leather to burn it dark. The slower the pen is moved, the darker the line will be, because the slower movement gives the pen a longer time to burn any given spot on the leather. Therefore, if the pen changes speed while drawing a line, the line will appear light and dark in places.

Avoid the temptation to burn too fast. The increased speed causes the lines to burn too light because the pen has not had contact long enough with the leather to burn it darker. If the temperature setting is then turned up to make the line darker, the setting may get so high that it makes the pen handle really hot and the burn consistency really hard to control. The fast speed results in lighter lines even though there is a high dial setting and the pen is faintly glowing. However, the high temperature will cause very dark marks whenever there is the slightest hesitation while burning. It's better to spend the majority of your burning time with a consistent, slower speed and adjust your temperature dial to change the tones from light to dark.

To achieve lines with consistent width and color:

- Have the pen in motion to draw the line as soon as the pen is put down on the material

- Draw the line at a consistent, somewhat slow speed

- End the line by simply lifting the pen when it gets to the end

Problem: blob at the start of the line.
Cause: setting the pen down on the leather and only then beginning to move the pen to draw the line.
Solution: start moving as soon as the pen touches leather.

Problem: blob at the end of the line.
Cause: drawing the line, then hesitating before lifting the pen off the leather.
Solution: lift the pen immediately upon finishing a line.

Problem: blob at both ends of the line.
Cause: starting and ending the line properly, but drawing too quickly, causing the line between the start and stop points to be too light.
Solution: slow down your drawing speed.

Problem: end of the line becomes thinner and disappears.
Cause: drawing a good line, but too quickly whisking the pen up at the end. (This is actually a good technique to use to create a thin end, such as the ends of whiskers.)
Solution: don't panic at the end of the line; practice calmly and smoothly finishing and lifting.

Problem: signature is not a consistent color.
Cause: changing speed while writing. Adults use a tempo when signing their name; usually slow for the first letter or two and then speeding up the rest of the name. If the change in tempo is used while burning the signature, the signature will be darker on the first few letters and very light for the rest of the name because of the change in speed.
Solution: sign more slowly than you would when writing with pen.

Pen Angles

When learning to burn on leather, hold the pyrography pen like a writing pen and observe the following angles to achieve the correct position.

Side-to-side angle: Avoid leaning the pen to the side in either direction. Leaning it to the side can change the width of the line, especially in a curve, resulting in an inconsistent burn.

Vertical angle: Observe how high or low you are holding the pen by looking at the angle from the table surface to the vertical position of the pen. The majority of the time, a comfortable 45° angle is used. There are times when raising the end of the pen to a more vertical position is useful to achieve a different mark with the pen, but it is tiring to hold the pen in a vertical position and it allows the heat to rise directly onto the fingers.

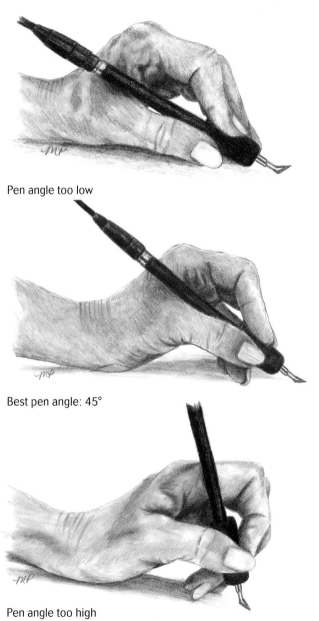

Pen angle too low

Best pen angle: 45°

As you can see, tilting the pen from side to side could affect the way this skew tip burns the leather.

Pen angle too high

Hand Support

Supporting your hand, even if it's just on the work surface, is essential.

Hand support is very important when burning because it gives you additional control over the pen. The easiest way to understand this concept is to imagine writing your signature by holding the pen without touching the paper. Your signature would not look the same as when you sign your name while resting your hand on the paper. Using a pyrography pen is similar. If you cannot rest your hand on the material's surface or support your hand, the outcome will be harder to control.

A support can make a big difference if you're using a solid point pen.

Supporting your hand on a piece of flat leather while burning with a wire tip pen is easily achieved by simply resting your pen hand on the leather. However, a solid point pen has a longer distance from where you hold the pen to the tip, which makes it hard to rest your hand on the leather and get some of the pen tips at the correct burning angle. Often pyrographers lean a solid point pen to the side to get the vertical high/low pen angle needed, but they sacrifice their side-to-side angle. The solution to achieve both angles while using a solid point pen is to elevate your pen hand by placing something under it, such as a piece of wood, a rolled sock, or your other hand/wrist.

Supporting your hand while burning on a piece of raised or modeled leather is more difficult with either type of pen. See the section "Working on a 3D Surface" on page 43 for more information on how to achieve hand support on a 3D surface.

Pen Pressure

Pressure can create wider lines with writer tips.

Pressure can also create wider lines with skew tips.

Pressure can even create molding.

Leather has a lot of elasticity and moves easily when pressure is applied while burning. Pressure affects burning in the following ways:

- Applying more pressure with a writer pen when drawing lines results in a wider line because the tip pressing on the leather causes it to push deeper into the leather and the leather is not only burning under the tip but on the sides of the depression as well.

- Applying more pressure with a skew pen when drawing lines results in a wider line because the skew tip is beveled, and as you push into the leather, it pushes the side walls of the channel farther apart while burning them.

- Applying more pressure with a shader pen can result in the molding of leather with the heat and pressure. See page 42 for more information.

Direction of Burning

Although pyrography pens can be used in any direction while burning the leather, there are instances when the direction you move the pen is important and, therefore, the project needs to be rotated to achieve the burn direction without contorting your hand or arm. Sometimes a piece is too large to be easily rotated, but if the leather can be turned, it should be done to keep your strokes consistent.

When burning a **frame pattern** that changes direction as it moves from horizontal to vertical, rotate the leather when it changes direction so you can comfortably continue to make your pen strokes.

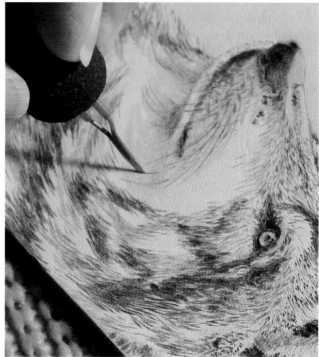
Burn hair or fur by rapidly whisking the tip up at the end of the line.

When burning **hair or whiskers**, the line is started like a normal line, but the end of the line is rapidly lifted. This whisking method causes the start of the line to be thicker and the end of the line to be thin. So, when a hair or whisker is drawn, the start of the line, which is thicker, should be on the face or body where it is attached, and the end of the line, which is thinner, should be off the face or body. Turn your project so that you can easily make this type of pen stroke in the fluid motion in the desired direction. I find it easiest to start the pen stroke on the head and then pull the pen toward my elbow on the arm holding the pen.

Start the stroke where it needs to be darker.

When shading an **even gradation from dark to light**, it is easier to move the pen in the same overlapping direction. I usually pull the shader from darkest to light in overlapping strokes. On wire tip burners, the shader is hotter when held in the air and cools rapidly once it comes in contact with the leather. Therefore, the shader naturally starts its stroke darker and, if left on the leather during its stroke, will get lighter and lighter. To take advantage of the fact that the stroke starts darker and gets lighter, rotate the project so you can start the stroke on the image where you want it to be its darkest and pull it in the direction it needs to be lighter.

Shade a shape from the outside in.

When **shading a shape** in your design or picture, keep the shader on the inside of the shape. For example, if you want to shade the inside of a circle, rotate the circle so you can put the toe of the shader on the line and have the rest of the shader on the inside of the circle. This way the shader is not blocking your view of the line and you can avoid possibly burning outside of the line.

Techniques for Different Pen Tip Types

See the "Pen Tip Categories" section on page 16 for information about how pen tips are categorized and their different characteristics. Each of the four categories—writer, skew, shader, and branding/specialty—has its own special needs and techniques.

Writers

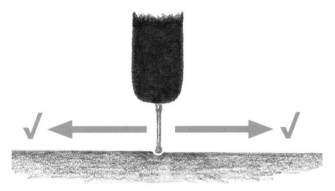

Writer pens can move in any direction.

Writer pens are designed with rounded edges on the tips to allow lines to be burned in a freeform style in any direction. Writers are useful when drawing circles and loops, like you do when writing. Writers draw on the surface of the leather, and, because of their rounded edges, the burn lines they produce have soft edges. These burned surface lines also tend to have a lighter brown or sometimes smeared appearance when compared to the lines a skew pen creates.

Hold a writer pen similar to a ballpoint pen. Avoid holding the end of the pen too high into a vertical position, because this allows the heat to rise onto your fingers. Light pressure when burning will produce a thinner line; applying more pressure when burning will produce a thicker line.

Your stroke direction simply follows the wire direction in a bent-wire writer.

When using a bent-wire writer, your pen stroke will be in the same direction as the wire is bent. Use the bent-wire pen for natural-looking lines and writing where slight thick and thin lines are desired. Depending on how wide or narrow the bend is in the wire, it will burn a thick and thin calligraphy effect when drawing circles. Bent-wire writers also produce dots that are more oval in shape to the degree the wire is bent.

Writer tips are great for dots and doodles.

Ball writers produce perfectly round dots and even lines, no matter which direction the pen is moving. Ball writers also leave tiny dots when the pen changes direction while scribbling, which can be helpful for texturing dog's noses or anything needing a bumpy texture appearance. Bent-wire writers, on the other hand, leave a smooth line appearance when scribbling.

Skews

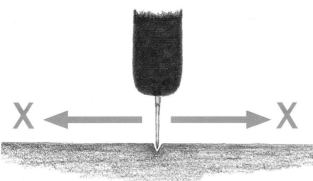

Skew pens cannot move sideways.

Skew pens have a knife tip, so they cut the leather while burning and ride slightly below the surface of the leather, making it impossible to make a circle in one motion. Because the knife tip is in the leather, it cannot move sideways without breaking or skipping across the leather. The only way to burn a circle with a skew tip is to burn the circle as a series of end-to-end short segments. Because skew pens burn into the leather, they burn lines with sharp edges and tend to burn dark brown or black in color. Skew pens are useful for burning coarse hair, edging larger letters, and anywhere that you desire clean, sharp edges and dark burning.

Like a writer pen, hold a skew pen as you would a ballpoint pen, avoiding a position where the end of the pen is too high in a vertical position. Using light pressure when burning will produce a thinner line; applying more pressure when burning will produce a thicker line.

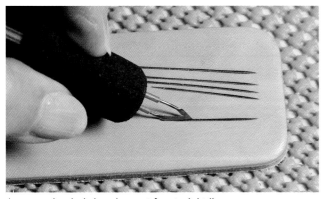

A square-heeled skew is great for straight lines.

The square-heeled skew is designed to make straight lines, although you can use it to make curved lines if you keep the heel off the leather. When using a square-heeled skew, start the stroke in motion, bringing the point down first followed by the heel while in motion, and then dropping the heel into the leather, continuing the burn in motion. Using this technique with a square-heeled skew will produce straight lines because the toe and heel in the leather make the tool self-tracking.

A round-heeled skew is good for curved lines.

The round-heeled skew is designed to make curved lines, although you can make short straight lines or use a metal ruler to make longer straight lines. When drawing a curved line, do not use your whole arm to make the stroke. Using your whole arm will allow the pen to curve in one direction, but your body will be in the way of you making a curved line in the other direction. Instead, make a curved line by holding the pen and twisting it in your fingers while you are pulling it. Depending on which way you twist the pen, the curve will go one way or another. Usually making a curve feels natural in one direction but awkward in the other. Practice twisting both ways to get comfortable with this technique.

Shaders

Shader tips allow you to create rich spectrums of color.

Shader pens allow you to add flat, smooth, burned "color" to a design or picture. Shading can be burned on leather using the bent, iron-like tips so that the burned color goes from dark to light in a gradual fade. This technique gives a subtle effect that cannot be achieved by using leather dyes or acrylics without airbrushing. The burned area created with a shader can be very pale to dark brown. A shader burns the surface of the leather, and, depending on the amount of pressure while burning, the surface of the leather may start separating with tiny flesh-toned cracks appearing under

magnification. The leather grain may also cause tiny underburned dots to show under magnification.

Shaders take a little more practice to use well compared to the other type of pen tips. In particular, the pen angle and direction you burn make a big difference. (Review the sections "Pen Angles" on page 32 and "Direction of Burning" on page 34).

One technique that is hard to master with a shader is the control of the pen temperature. With a one-temperature solid point burner, the difficulty is creating lighter burns, which is achieved by burning faster or burning while the pen is heating up or cooling down. Practice on a test piece while focusing on the speed and/ or the window of the right temperature while heating up/cooling down the pen.

With a wire tip burner, the challenge is keeping the tip hot once it starts burning the leather. Because the nichrome wire tips heat up and cool down so quickly, they are very sensitive to environmental changes in temperature. While the tip is in the air, it can get as hot as the temperature dial setting, but as soon as the tip comes in contact with the leather, the cool surface will drop the tip temperature significantly. The result is usually a dark burned blob when the tip touches the material surface, followed by a change in burn color to a very light burn and the inability to get the shader to burn dark. There are a couple of ways to change your technique to avoid this issue.

Short, overlapping strokes are the way to achieve a nice, even fill.

Using a circular motion can create a nice cloud/smoke effect.

- Once the shader pen tip is hot, lower it to the leather surface and breeze over the area you are going to burn, barely touching the surface. I call this "lightly tickling the surface." This technique starts cooling down the tip. After a couple of "tickling" strokes, bring the shader down on the surface in motion. If you are trying to achieve a smooth, even shaded area, make the strokes short and repeat the next stroke starting at the same location, but moving the pen over slightly so the next stroke is overlapping. When you want longer strokes, burn a row of short strokes and then burn the second row of short strokes that overlap the first row. Keep repeating this technique until you fill in the desired area. By making the strokes short, it allows the pen's temperature to start recovering from the dropped temperature caused by the cool leather surface.

- If your shading gets too light while burning, hold the tip up in the air for a second to let the tip recuperate its heat.

- Since it is very hard to correct mistakes on leather, it is better to burn a little light and then add darker burns than it is to burn too dark and then try to lighten your burn.

- Avoid holding the shader pen in one place on the leather to burn it darker. The prolonged, stationary contact will result in leather debris becoming stuck to the shader tip. If this happens, use a razor blade as described on page 25 to remove the debris.

- If your shaded area appears uneven in tone and you wanted an even, smooth burn, you can fix the unevenness by using a level-setting technique; see the "Leveling an Uneven Shaded Area" section on page 49.

- A circular motion can also be used when burning with a shader. This technique produces a modeled, fluffy shading similar to clouds or smoke, depending on the size of the circular motion and the leather surface. Practice playing with this technique for shading these types of textures.

Different Types of Shading

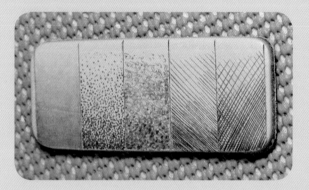

Shader pens are designed to produce **flat, tonal shading**. Tones are the different shades of the browns and blacks that burning produces. However, there are other methods of shading that can be achieved using both writer and skew pens. You can add shading using a writer pen by **stippling** (creating overlapping dots) or **scribbling** (creating overlapping looping circles, similar to writing "e"s or "o"s). If you overlap the scribbles or dots a lot, the result will be darker shading. Conversely, if you don't overlap the circles and dots a lot, the result will be lighter shading. You can also create shading using either writers or skews by creating parallel lines. This method is called **hatching** (parallel lines in one direction) or **cross-hatching** (parallel lines in two different directions). If the lines are closer together, the shading will appear darker; if the lines are further apart, the shading will appear lighter.

Branding/Specialty

This is a realistic scale effect achieved with a branding tip.

Branding/specialty pens allow the burning of shapes and patterns by holding the hot tip on the leather using a branding technique. Branding tips are very similar to leather stamping tools, except you are using heat and pressure. The resulting burn can texture the leather surface depending on how much heat and pressure are used.

Lettering Techniques

There are a couple of methods for adding lettering to a leather project.

You can simply **use a writer to burn hand-drawn letters**. You can use a soft pencil (2B to 9B hardness) to sketch your lettering beforehand so that you can evenly space what you will be burning. I use this method when I want to create small lettering that looks handwritten.

Lettering can be transferred like any pattern.

You can also **transfer the letters as a pattern**. For this technique, first create the lettering on your computer by typing out the words or phrases. Then modify the font, size, and letter spacing to look exactly how you want the final lettering to appear. Then print the formatted lettering on plain paper to use as a transfer pattern. Transfer the pattern onto your leather using the dry method (see page 27).

Draw the outline of the letter with a writer pen first.

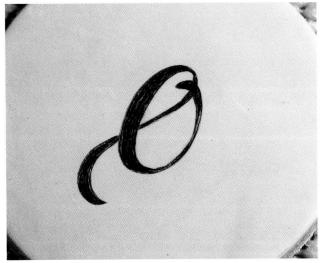
The finished letter, crisp and clean.

Sometimes when transferring the letters as patterns, your transfer line is not exactly on the edge of the letter, which can give you an O with a bump on the curve of the letter or a letter E with a crooked spine, for example. By drawing the lines around the letters lightly with a writer pen first, you can work out the discrepancies of the transferred letters. Then go back over the letters darker to fill them in. Don't forget to erase the graphite transfer lines and touch up any mistakes (see page 47).

When I am transferring larger letters that I want very sharp and dark, I use the transfer method as previously described, outlining the letters very lightly with a writer pen to get the shape of the letter worked out and then filling in the letters with the writer pen. Then I use a skew pen and re-burn the letter edges, very slowly and meticulously, using magnifying glasses.

Tip:

To bend computer-generated lettering to fit in a curved area, print the letters and closely trim around them. Create slits on the top and bottom of the paper between each letter, cutting deep but not all the way through the center. Bend the text to fit the curve. Trim or overlap the paper edges so each letter shows fully. Tape the curved text down using clear tape and photocopy the bent text to create a fresh pattern for transfer.

Texturing and "Embossing" with Heat

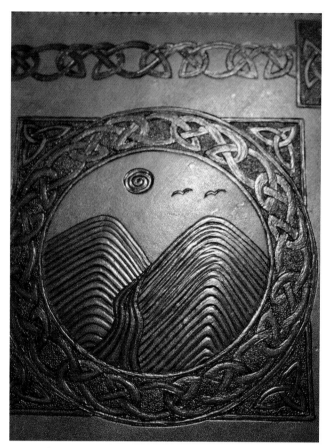

One of the coolest characteristics of pyrography is the ability to use heat and pressure to texture the material. On leather, the texturing is minimal to none if the leather is thin, but thicker leather textures well. Texture can be created by pushing a writer tip into the leather or pressing and cutting the leather with a skew tip. By repeating these techniques in a large area, you will create more texture, giving your piece a very tactile feel. If you cut a line with a skew pen and then press a shader pen along the cut line, you will get a neat embossed effect. The heat from the shader pen "molds" the leather.

Burning and Tooling

When possible, complete any leather tooling, embossing, or modeling before you burn the leather. These processes require wetting/casing the leather. After the leather tooling, embossing, or modeling is complete, let the leather dry completely before you burn.

When using writer or shader pens to burn leather, the burn is on the surface of the leather. Once the leather is burned, the rubbing action of casing, tooling, embossing, or modeling can lighten the original burn, which is why it is better to do your burning after you use these leathercrafting methods.

If you have burned the leather and then decide to add tooling, embossing, or modeling, you can do this to an area that is unburned. Start by wetting/casing the leather. You'll need to wet the leather all over, including the burned area, so the leather retains a consistent color. When wetting the burned area, mist the area with a sprayer or dab it with a sponge, but do not rub the pyrography.

Working on a 3D Surface

Burning on a raised, 3D surface is more challenging than burning on a flat surface. Even though it makes burning more difficult, you still want to tool, emboss, or model the leather into a raised surface before burning. If you burn the leather first and then try to reshape the surface into a 3D structure, the process will lighten the burning. (See the previous section, Burning and Tooling.)

The main challenges when working on a raised, 3D surface are:

- Maintaining hand support

- Controlling the pen angles

- Managing the pen in convex, concave, and tight areas

Maintaining Hand Support

Maintaining a supported hand position is important to controlling the pen and, therefore, your burning. (See the section "Hand Support" on page 33.) How you want to handle hand support on a 3D project is going to depend on how large the project is. A technique typically used by woodcarvers for supporting the pen hand while working on 3D objects is to place the pinky finger on the object while holding the pen above the surface with the rest of the fingers. This allows the flexibility to position the pen at various angles while the pinky finger remains on the surface at a stationary point, yet retaining the ability to pivot so that the change in pen angles can be accommodated. If you are not used to doing this method, your pinky finger may get sore after extended burning. This will pass after the muscles in your finger become strengthened over time.

If the 3D object is relatively flat but on a curved surface, a method that works well is to support the pen hand by building up the surface under the hand so the hand is at the same height as the surface you are burning. For example, if you want to burn on a ball, you can put an object (block of wood, rolled washcloth, etc.) under your pen hand so your hand is resting at the same height as the top of the ball. This method allows you to rotate the ball while your hand is on the support so you can burn on all sides of the ball as you rotate it. You can use a beanbag or non-slip material under the ball to keep it from rolling out of position.

Controlling the Pen Angles

Keep the pen angled at 45° to the surface.

Burn the channels with a writer pen.

Controlling the pen angles, both horizontal and vertical, are difficult as you move the pen over the changing 3D surface. (Review the "Pen Angles" section on page 32.) As you are burning the 3D surface, adjust your pen angle to remain upright, not leaning too much to the left or right, and at the 45° vertical angle in relation to the surface plane at each moment. To accomplish this, your hand must be fluid and change angles to mirror the changes in the surface. Depending on the object's shape and size, you may need to rotate the object when following the flow of the surface planes while burning.

Managing the Pen in Convex, Concave, and Tight Areas

Burn the tops of the ridges with a shader pen.

On a complex 3D surface, it may become challenging to burn in tight areas and steep convex and concave areas due to the size of your tools. Sometimes you'll need to burn what you can in the areas where your tools can reach and then burn the areas your pen could not reach using a smaller pen. For example, if you are trying to burn two ridges and there is a deep channel between them, you should burn the ridge tops first with a shader and then burn the narrow channel with the side of a writer or skew, as you start from the bottom of the channel while lifting and scraping the sides of the wall. Sometimes, at the bottom of a U-shaped channel, you can use a writer to burn the bottom of the channel. There are also a variety of miniature pyrography pens available to help burn in these tight areas. It helps when burning in close spaces to turn your temperature down so you can move slower and to use magnification so you can place the pen tip in its exact position to burn where you want without overburning the area around it.

Tonal Values

Pyrography is monochromatic (one color), so it's important to understand how to vary the intensity of the burned color to create and define the image. Without contrast between light and dark tones (different shades of the browns and blacks that burning produces), the aspects of a picture blend together and the image becomes muddy. Using a tonal scale can improve your pyrography.

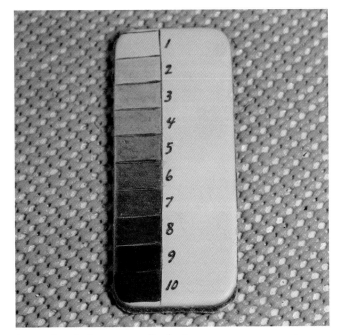

A tonal scale is a gauge displaying an even progression from light to dark rendered in a set of numbered steps, usually 5 or 10 steps. Using only a few tones in the middle of the scale (around 4 to 6 on a 10-step scale) leads to artwork with no real emphasis. To create some drama, use middle-valued tones along with some tones at the beginning and end of the scale—adding a range will change your piece for the better. Placing a light tone against a dark one draws the viewer's attention and emphasizes a focal point in a piece.

When artwork has all of its tonal values at the lighter end of the tonal scale, it is referred to as "high key." Conversely, if the tones are all from the darker end of the tonal scale, it is labeled "low key." If the artwork has tonal values from all over the tonal scale (light, middle, and dark) it is in "full contrast." Use high and low key to set a mood, such as a bright sunny day or a dark scary scene, and use full contrast to create dramatic artwork.

Making a Tonal Scale

To make a tonal scale, cut a piece of the same leather you will be using to burn your project. Draw lines to create 10 squares at least ½" (1.3cm) wide. Label the squares 1 to 10. Leave the first square unburned. This is your lightest light. Your scale can be filled in to match the shading technique you will be using on your project, whether using a shader, a stippling technique with a writer, or a hatching/cross-hatching technique with a skew. Fill the last square, square 10, with the darkest burn you can create without scorching the unburned leather next to the square. Next, fill square 2 with the lightest burn you can achieve. Fill square 3 with a slightly darker burn than square 2. Continue until you fill square 9. It's best to make small, incremental changes as you fill each square, which will allow you to adjust the tones once you reach square 9. It's always easier to adjust the scale and burn the squares a little darker if you get to square 9 and decide that it's too big of a tonal change between squares 9 and 10.

Judging Tonal Depth

To test whether you are using a full tonal scale and the objects in the artwork are well defined, look at your artwork from 5' to 8' (1.5 to 2.5m) away. If the elements of your artwork are blending together, or if the most prominent features are not noticeable, then you need to add more tonal depth to your artwork. Another method to determine if you are using a full tonal scale is to squint your eyes and evaluate your artwork for contrast and definition.

Using a Tonal Scale

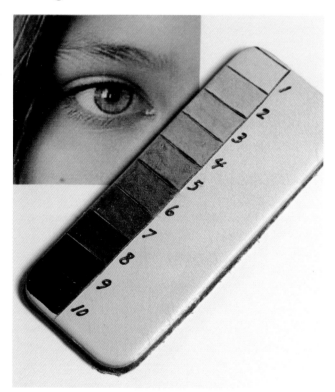

Whether you are basing a pyrography project on a photograph or a shaded drawing, the easiest way to match it to a tonal scale is to start by printing or photocopying a grayscale or sepia (brown shades only) version of the reference photo or drawing.

Make a tonal scale, hold it next to each area in the photo/drawing, and determine which numbered square on the scale most closely matches that area. Then burn that area on the project to match the darkness of the corresponding square on the scale. If you are working with a color photograph or drawing, match the tonal scale to the colors in the image by squinting your eyes so the objects in the photo/drawing are out of focus. While squinting, slide the scale next to each object and decide which square on the tonal scale blends best with its value. Write the tonal values on the grayscale copy for reference while you are burning the project.

When you are assigning tonal values, consider three factors:

- The base color of an object (see below)
- The highlights
- The shadows

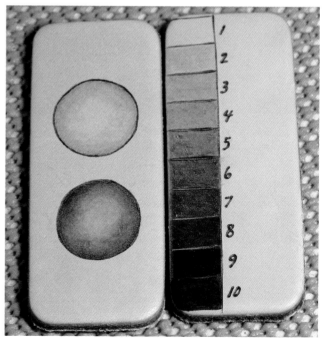

For example, if you are burning a picture of a red ball and a yellow ball, the base color of the red ball may match 6 on the tonal scale, while its highlights may match 3 to 4 and the shadows match 7 to 8. However, the base color of the yellow ball may match 2, whereas its highlights may be 1 and the shadows match 3 to 4. You need to match and mark all of these tonal values to create a realistic burning. The highlights appear where the light source shines on the objects, and will be burned with the lighter tones on the tonal scale. Reflections or glares are even lighter than highlights, and will match square 1, the lightest value (unburned leather).

One method to create a burning with full contrast is to burn almost everything in the picture with light and middle tonal values, leaving the lightest areas as square 1 (unburned). Once the rest of the picture is burned in light and middle tones, determine which areas need to be burned darker—from the middle tones all the way to square 10, the darkest tone. With the addition of the darkest tones, your picture will be in full contrast and will be more dramatic.

Touching Up Mistakes

Leather does not lend itself to being easily corrected. If you scrape away the burn to fix a mistake, it is very easy to scrape too much and leave a very light mark on the leather that will show. Therefore, when you burn on leather, you need to take your time and be very careful. It is best to **leave all touch-ups until the end of the project** because sometimes mistakes are covered up by additional burning or you may decide to make that area darker later. You want to avoid touching up a mistake and then deciding later to make that area darker and end up reburning over a place you already took the time to touch up.

Touching Up a Burn Mistake

When you make a mistake, first **assess whether the design can be altered** to hide the mistake. You may be able to add a few elements like extra leaves if you are working on a tree. You may also be able to add a background pattern. If a redesign is not possible, then touch up the mistake using a razor blade as follows.

Oops, a mistake: the shader burned outside the line.

Lightly scrape the offending area with a razor blade.

Stop scraping when you have achieved the base leather color.

Scraping too much will result in a patch that is lighter than the base leather.

- Use a strong magnifier (magnifying glasses or table attachment) to do this process, because you need to see more closely what you are fixing than your naked eyes can see.

- Using a single-edge razor blade as a scraper, lightly scrape the burn you are fixing. Keep the razor blade very flat to the surface and only lift the end of the razor blade so you don't scrape the whole width of the blade. Do not use just the corner point of the razor blade because it will gouge the leather. Use it like you would scrape the burn off a piece of toast—the blade low across the surface but using only the end of one side. Tilt the razor blade and scrape in the direction in which the top of the razor blade is leaning. Do not scrape the leather around the mistake, because it will turn the leather a lighter color.

- Only scrape the burn to the point that its color matches the surrounding leather. If you continue further, the leather's outermost surface will be removed and the lighter color under it will show. If that happens, as a last resort, you try a very difficult touch up—you can use a "two hair" paintbrush (a very, very fine paintbrush) and dot the lighter spot with a very diluted acrylic wash (leather color) to touch it up. Note that the wet touched-up spot will be lighter when it dries, which makes it difficult to match. It's better to start lighter than you think and let it dry to see the resulting color.

Leveling an Uneven Shaded Area

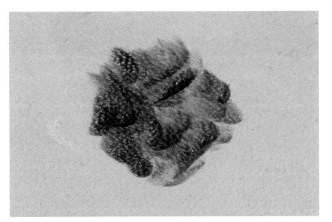

This uneven shading needs to be fixed up.

Burn the lighter spots darker.

- Use a strong magnifier (magnifying glasses or table attachment) to do this process, because you need to see more closely what you are fixing than your naked eyes can see.

- Assess the shaded area for which spots are lighter tones, middle tones, and darker tones. For this process, you will be darkening the lighter tones and lightening the darker tones until they are all the same as the original middle tones. The end result will be an evenly shaded area.

- Using a shader on low heat, very lightly burn the areas that are lighter in color. Make sure not to burn into the surrounding middle and dark tones, or you'll make the problem worse. When shading the lighter area, bring the shader tip down in motion and lift up in motion before you get to the end of the lighter area. This will fade the additional shading both on the start and end of the touch-up stroke.

Scrape the darkest spots lighter.

- Using a single-edge razor blade, as mentioned in the "Touching Up Mistakes" section on page 47, very lightly scrape the darker areas until the color of the darker areas matches the middle tone. Make sure not to scrape into the surrounding middle tones, or you'll make the problem worse.

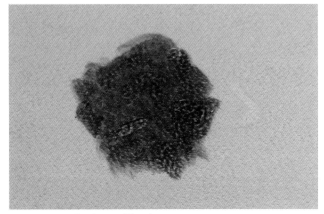

Now the tone is nice and level.

Chapter 4

COLOR AND FINISH

Adding Color to Pyrography

Color can be added to pyrography using many different mediums—leather dyes and acrylics, traditional artist dyes and paints, wax- and oil-based colored pencils, or markers. Which medium you choose to use and how much color pigment you apply will give your project a different look, from subtle color to dramatic saturated color.

Colored with water-based leather dyes

Colored with wax-based colored pencils

Colored with acrylic washes

Colored with permanent markers

Applying Color

Always burn your design before you apply color.

When using any of these color mediums, you need to burn your image first and then add the color. You do not want to color first and then burn, because you would be burning the color pigment instead of burning the leather; you would definitely smell the fumes of the burning pigment. Your leather must also be completely dry (such as after any leather tooling you added) before you add color.

Dyes and markers will soak into the leather and won't cover the burned image. Acrylics, oils, and watercolor will not cover the burned area if you thin the paints into a wash and apply them sparingly when going over the burned image. If you use the paints thicker than a wash, you will cover the burned image when you paint over it. Too thick and the paint can crack and peel over time on pieces that are handled or bent often. Wax-based and oil-based colored pencils will also cover the burned areas. Therefore, if you use thicker pigmented paints or colored pencils, you will need to color around or up to the edge of any burned areas (assuming you want your hard work to be visible!).

Dyes can be purchased as water-based dyes or solvent-based dyes. Both types of dyes can be diluted using water or solvent, respectively. Acrylics and watercolors are water-based and can be diluted with water. Oils are solvent-based and can be diluted using appropriate solvents. Dyes and paints, whether water-based or solvent-based, can also be mixed to create new colors.

Dyes and paint washes can be applied to the leather using paintbrushes, wool daubers (wool balls on the end of a metal wire handle), felt daubers, or cotton swabs, or by airbrushing or spraying.

Dyes and markers, especially the solvent-based kind, can spread when applied. In order to stop the dye from spreading past the intended area, color close to but not all the way up against the line or edge of the shape and let the natural tendency to spread take the dye the rest of the way to the edge of the line or shape.

Artist quality colored pencils apply more pigment than inexpensive colored pencils and can be wax-based or oil-based, whereas inexpensive colored pencils are usually wax-based and have less pigment. Any colored pencil can be applied in multiple layers to obtain a more intense color. You can seal each layer of color by spraying a workable fixative spray, a UV filter spray, or a coat of clear acrylic spray. Colored pencils can leave a lot of dust residue while coloring. Keep excess residue cleared off the leather with a large, dry paintbrush or a horsehair brush. The waxy residue can also get trapped in burned skew cuts and obscure the burn. You can eliminate the residue in the cuts by applying heat from a hairdryer and rubbing over the skew cut with a cotton swab. Cotton swabs can also smooth and blend the color from wax-based colored pencils when heat is applied with the hairdryer.

Test, Test, Test Your Color

Testing on matching leather shows the final color.

Vegetable-tanned leather turns darker and forms a patina when exposed to sunlight, but it bleaches lighter when exposed to extreme amounts of sunlight. (See the section "Color and Finish Testing" on page 54.) Dyes and markers allow the leather to show through so the color will change as the leather forms a patina. Also, when dyes and markers are applied to leather, the result can be darker than when they are applied to other types of materials. Dyes and paints also produce different coloring effects when diluted to different strengths and layered with multiple coatings.

Whichever colors and mediums you decide to use on your finished piece must be tested on a scrap piece of leather with the same leather darkness (patina) as the leather your project is made from. This testing will give you a true representation of what the color will do when added to your project. Skipping this test may result in you being unhappy with a project that you spent a lot of time and materials to create.

Color Usage

Spot color can distract you from the important objects.

Before you start adding color to a project, take the time to pick the palette of colors you will use and decide how much of the image you will be coloring. There are a lot of books and information about choosing and mixing colors that complement each other and how colors affect the mood, symbolism, balance, and movement of a piece. Understand that coloring a single object in an image can draw the viewer's eye to that object, making it the focal point of the image. For example, if you burn an image of a dog near a ball, and then you decide to only add color to the ball, the viewer's eye will go straight to the ball and not the dog. This will make the ball the focal point of the image, not the dog.

Adding Finish to Pyrography

To seal and protect your pyrography work and leather, you will want to add a finish over the leather. There are many leather finish products on the market to seal and protect your work.

Leather resists are leather finishes that are used to seal the leather and prevent additional dyes, stains, and paints from changing anything the resist has sealed. Leather resists can be applied over leather that you have added color to or natural leather. When the leather has color applied, it is best to let it dry overnight so that the color is completely dry before you apply the resist. Two coats of a resist work better to seal what is underneath. Let each coat dry before applying the next coat. Tan-Kote creates a semi-opaque seal, which allows tainting of the leather or colors underneath by additional stains or dyes. Examples of leather resists include: Fiebing's brand Resolene and Tan-Kote; Tandy brand Eco-Flo® Super Shene® and Eco-Flo Satin Shene®.

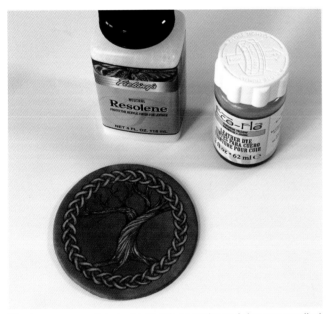

The image was painted with Resolene resist and dye was applied over it.

Leather antique stains and gels are applied over the entire surface and then wiped off to leave some of the stain or gel to highlight leather tooling. These products obscure pyrography. If you want to use these stains and gels to highlight leather tooling on a piece with pyrography, consider using a leather resist to seal the pyrography to protect it from a stain or gel application. Examples of leather antique stains and gels include: Tandy brand Antique Leather Stain and Eco-Flo Gel Antique; Fiebing's brand Antique Leather Stain and Antique Finish.

Leather finishes are applied to seal the leather and color if it has been used. Let any applied color dry completely before adding a leather finish over it. Examples of leather finishes include: Fiebing's brand Tan-Kote, Saddle Lac, and Hi-Liter; Tandy brand

Neat-Lac® Leather Finish, Eco-Flo Super Shene, Eco-Flo Satin Shene, and Eco-Flo Carnauba Cream.

Finishes like Saddle Lac will protect the leather.

Leather conditioners keep the leather soft, pliable, and protected. These conditioners are best used over leather that has not been colored. Leather finishes can be applied over leather conditioners (except for products containing lacquer or that are very waxy, such as Tandy's Neat-Lac or Dr. Jackson's Hide Rejuvenator). Examples of leather conditioners include: Fiebing's brand Saddle Soap, Prime Neatsfoot Oil Compound, Snow-Proof Weatherproofing Paste, Leather Balm, and Mink Oil; Dr. Jackson's brand Waterproof Wax and Hide Rejuvenator; Lexol® brand Cleaner and Conditioner; Tandy brand Carnauba Cream.

Leather burnishers, like gum tragacanth, are used to smooth down the fibers prior to burnishing the edge with an edge burnisher (a round plastic or wooden tool with smooth grooves to rub along the edges). **Leather edge finishes** are used to seal the cut, exposed edges on your leather pieces to give them a finished appearance. Examples of leather burnishers and leather edge finishes include: Fiebing's brand Edge Kote; Tandy brand Eco-Flo Gum Tragacanth.

Test, Test, Test Your Finish

If you have added any color to the leather, you should test your finish over the type of color that you used to ensure the color does not run and smear when your finish is applied over the top. Do this on a scrap piece of leather with the same color added.

Color and Finish Testing

In the interest of documenting the interaction of sunlight on various pyrography pens, techniques, colors, and finishes, I created a controlled experiment. Depending on what tools and products you want to use, you may benefit from my work or want to run your own tests. The only way to be reasonably sure of a final result is to test it first!

I created three identical leather panels with different pyrography pens and coloring in each column:

- Column 1 has burned marks from a writer pen.

- Column 2 has burned marks from a skew pen.

- Column 3 has burned coloring created from a shader pen.

- Column 4 has yellow and blue water-based leather dye applied.

- Column 5 has red, purple, and white acrylic paint applied.

- Column 6 has yellow, green, purple, hot pink, and orange permanent markers applied.

- Column 7 has red, light blue, lime green, and white Prismacolor® colored pencils applied (wax-based colored pencils).

- Column 8 has no color, but the column was half-blocked from the sun.

Different finishing products were then applied in rows across each column. The last column had a heavy poster board cover attached to block half of the last column to check the sun's effect using different finishes:

- Row 1 has an application of Tan-Kote.

- Row 2 has an application of Resolene.

- Row 3 has an application of Antique Finish.

- Row 4 has an application of Gel Antique.

- Row 5 has an application of Carnauba Cream.

- Row 6 has an application of Weatherproofing.

- Row 7 has an application of Leather Balm.

- Row 8 has an application of Super Shene.

- Row 9 has an application of Satin Shene.

- Row 10 has an application of Saddle Lac.

- Row 11 has an application of Spar Urethane (a wood product).

One panel was then designated the control and was placed in a box in a rarely opened dark closet to retain the characteristics of the initial applications. The second panel was designated Partial Sun and was taped to a south-facing window that was under a porch. The third panel was designated Full Sun and was taped to a west-facing window to capture the daily blazing sun of the Southeastern United States. At the end of nine months (from the beginning of June through the end of February), the panels were removed from their locations and assessed. The results are shown on these pages.

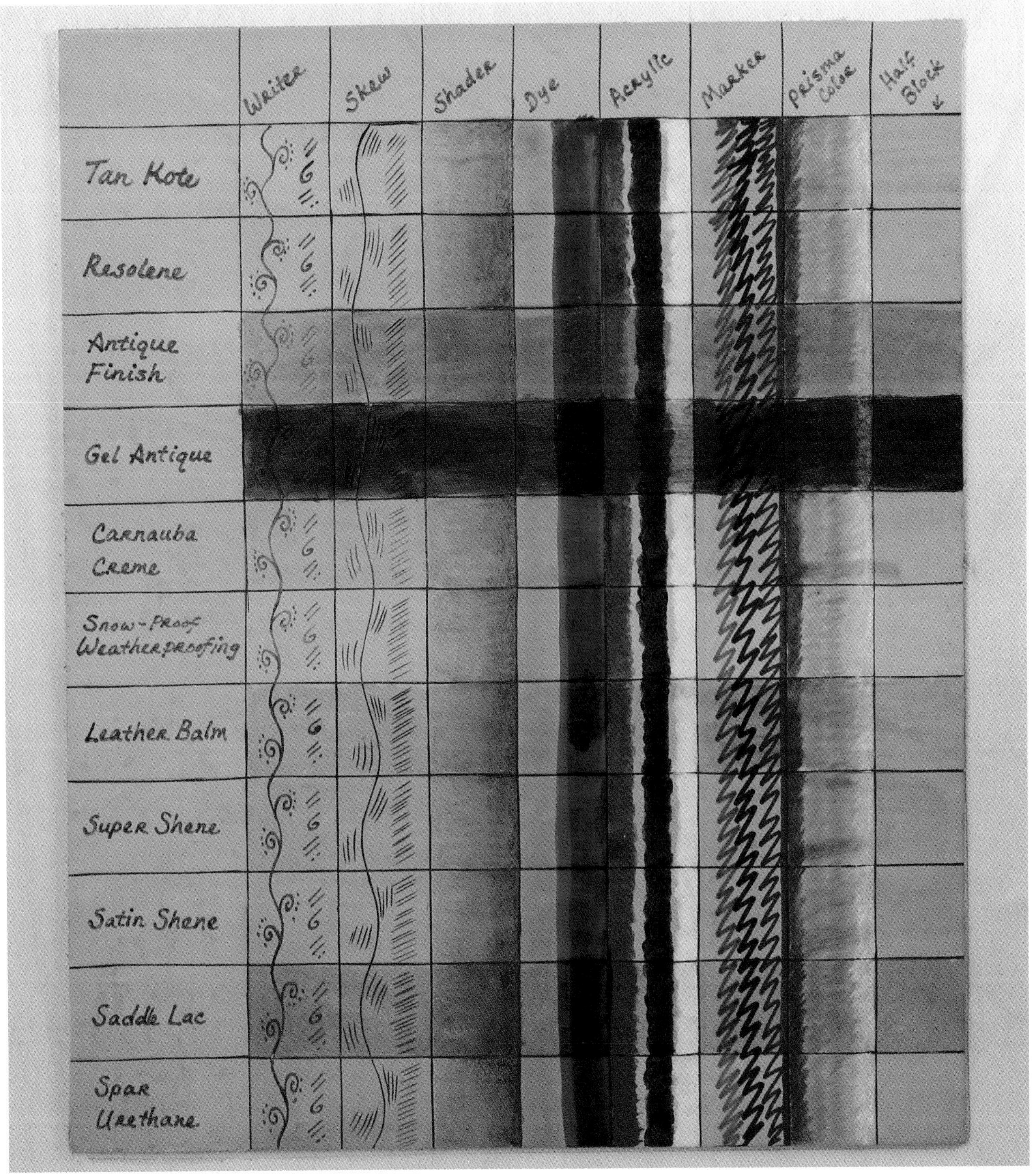

The control panel (stored in a closet for nine months).

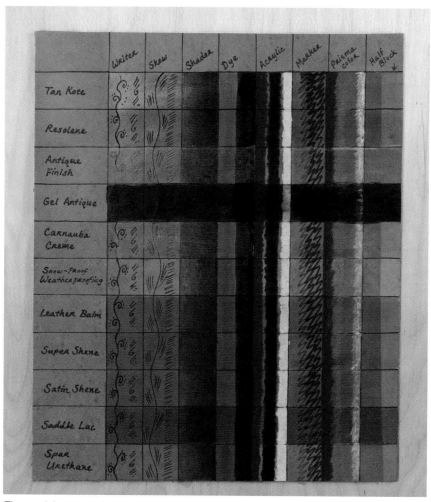

The partial sun panel.

My observations from these tests include the following:

- The pyrography did not fade or lighten on the leather like it would have on wood, even on the Full Sun test. The written row and column labels look the same on the Control panel, Partial Sun panel, and Full Sun panel.

- The leather water-based dyes and permanent markers faded and changed color with more exposure to sunlight, despite any of the finish products applied over them.

- The yellow dye and marker almost disappeared or completely disappeared using any of the finishes.

- The blue dye lost its intensity on the Partial Sun panel and faded to a blue-gray color when exposed on the Full Sun panel. The purple marker turned light pink on the Partial Sun panel and almost disappeared as very light pink on the Full Sun panel.

- I have had several projects using dyes and markers look the same years after they were created, but they were not exposed to as much sunlight as the Partial Sun or Full Sun test panels.

- The acrylic paint and Prismacolor pencils held their original colors despite the sun exposure.

- The application of Carnauba Cream, Leather Balm, Super Shene, and Satin Shene with a wool dauber smeared the leather dye and permanent markers.

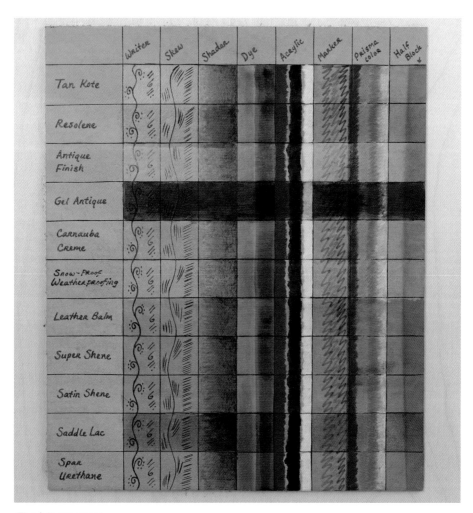

The full sun panel.

- Applying Tan-Kote and Resolene smeared the dyes and markers to a lesser degree.

- The Antique Finish turned a peachy-orange color on the Control panel, which also affected the colors. With Partial Sun exposure, it started turning into a whitish haze. With Full Sun exposure, it turned even whiter.

- The Gel Antique finish colored everything on its row a reddish-brown color. With Partial Sun exposure, it started turning a darker brown, hiding most colors. With Full Sun exposure, it faded to expose more colors but remained a dark brown.

- All finishes that were half-blocked by the poster board in the last column showed dramatic changes in the color of the leather from the effects of the sun, both on the Partial Sun panel and the Full Sun panel. This means that no matter which of these finishes you use, if you cover part of the leather with something that blocks the sun, a color change will show on the leather depending on what was exposed to the sun and what was not.

- The uncolored, unfinished leather was light on the Control panel. The leather turned darker when it had Partial Sun exposure, but lightened again when the Full Sun was able to bleach the leather.

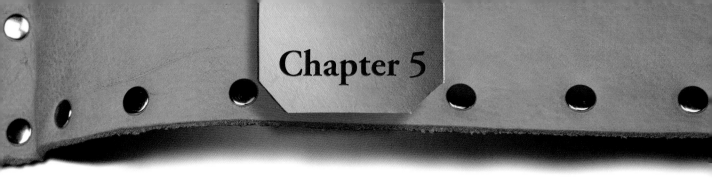

Chapter 5

PROJECTS

Coaster

Level: Beginner

Vegetable-tanned leather cutouts are available for purchase in many shapes. For example, there are round shapes used for coasters, ornaments, and embellishments to attach to objects; long rectangular shapes used for bookmarks and bracelets; small rectangular shapes used for barrettes, luggage tags, and embellishments; ovals used for belt buckle inserts; and key fob shapes. You can also purchase vegetable-tanned leather to cut your own unique shapes. This coaster, the key fob on page 64, and the bookmark on page 70 are all worked on premade leather cutouts and all use the same pattern in different ways. The pattern can be used without alteration across the entire cutout, or just parts of the pattern can be selected and used on the cutout—either with or without additional pattern parts or with the addition of text or lettering. See page 124 for the full Woodland pattern to use in this manner.

Note: Before getting started, test out the pattern on a scrap piece of leather. If you are having difficulty with the small shapes, you can enlarge the pattern before you transfer it onto your project.

Materials and Tools

- Vegetable-tanned leather coasters, 3¼" (8.3cm) in diameter (you can cut coasters from a leather hide using a metal food can as a template)
- Coaster pattern (page 126)
- Color in your preferred medium (optional)
- Edge burnisher and gum tragacanth or mink oil paste
- Your preferred finish
- Pyrography burner
- Small writer and small shader pen tips
- Unwaxed graphite paper
- Non-slip shelving liner
- White rubber/plastic eraser or artist kneaded eraser
- Razor blade
- Tape
- Painter's tape
- Pen
- Scissors

1 **Prepare.** Make a copy of the Coaster pattern on page 126. Tape a piece of non-slip shelving liner to your table. Place a dry vegetable-tanned round cutout close to the top edge of the liner with the grain (smooth) side up.

Tip:

Using a red pen helps you see where you traced. Check the transfer after a few minutes to see if the graphite paper is transferring onto the leather and not the back of the pattern.

Tip:

The graphite from your transferred pattern can build up on your pen tip, causing uneven leather burning. To avoid the excess graphite buildup, wipe your pen tip often on a piece of denim.

2

Transfer the pattern. Position the pattern over the coaster and tape one side of the pattern to the table in two places with painter's tape. Place unwaxed graphite paper between the pattern and the leather with the graphite side down. Trace the pattern onto the dry leather.

Burn the stems, leaves, and berries. Following the pattern lines, burn the stems and leaves using a small writer or skew pen. The writer pen is a little easier for beginners due to the pattern having a lot of curves. Test which pen you want to use on a scrap piece of leather because once you start burning, you should stay with the same pen to keep the lines consistent. I used a 0.8mm (1⁄32") ball writer. Avoid pressing hard while burning because it makes the lines wider, filling in the leaves. Burn the berries using the point of a writer pen.

Burn the rabbit. Continue to burn the rabbit that you transferred from the pattern using the small writer pen.

Add shading to stems and leaves. Using a small shader pen, add some light shading to the stems and leaves. I used a small round-toe shader and held it more vertical than usual to add shading in small places. Turn your project so that the shader is on the inside of the shape with the toe of the shader on the inside edge of the line. For the stems, I held the shader upright and ran it parallel to the stem line. For the leaves, I held the shader upright and ran it parallel to the leaf edge, starting at the stem and then fading while lifting when I got halfway down the leaf. I repeated the same technique running the toe of the shader down the leaf vein (center line on the leaf), from the stem to halfway down the leaf. The result is that the leaf will be darker next to the stem and lighter toward the end.

Add shading to the rabbit. Using the same shader pen, add shading to the rabbit while referring to the pattern. Turn your project so that the shader is on the inside of the shape with the toe of the shader on the inside edge of the line. Try the shader pen on a piece of scrap leather. If you are having difficulty with the shader pen, you can also shade using a stippling or scribbling technique described in the "Different Types of Shading" sidebar on page 39.

Clean up. Erase all of the transfer lines. Use the edge of a razor blade to lightly scrape any edges that are bumpy and any dark splotches in the shading. See the section "Touching Up Mistakes" on page 47. If you are adding color to your project, the color will hide some of the thicker lines inside the leaves, so you will not need to touch them up.

Tip:

When using an acrylic wash, do not overload the paintbrush. After thinning the acrylic paint with water, I only put enough paint on the brush to be a little more than dry brushing the paint. If you have too much water or paint on your brush, offload some of it on a paper towel. I also try to leave the burn showing so the leaves are a mix of green and brown, which makes them more realistic. To achieve this effect, I concentrate on adding the color to the ends of the leaves and then blend it into the brown toward the stem.

Add color (optional). If you wish, add color to your project. You can choose from any of the color mediums in the "Adding Color to Pyrography" section on page 50. Test all the colors you are going to use on a scrap piece of leather. I used an acrylic wash of olive green on the leaves, a pink marker over the berries, and a yellow marker on the butterfly.

Add finish. Once your color is dry, you can finish the edges of your cutout. Wet the edge of the cutout or apply a product such as gum tragacanth or mink oil paste, making sure you do not get any of it on the front or back of the cutout. Then use an edge burnisher on the edge by rubbing the burnisher back and forth until the edge is smooth. After testing the effects of your finish over your color on a scrap piece of leather, apply the finish to your project to protect the leather.

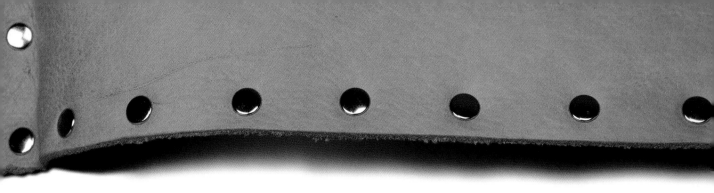

Key Fob

Level: Beginner

Key fobs come in different shapes when purchased as a cutout or kit. If the Key Fob pattern provided for this project doesn't fit your cutout, you can use pieces of the full-page Woodland pattern on page 124. Make a copy of the full-page pattern and cut out the pieces you want to use. Tape these pieces into position to fit your key fob cutout and then make a copy so your pattern is on a sheet of paper with no overlaps or tape to interfere with the transfer.

Materials and Tools

- Vegetable-tanned leather key fob, approx. 2⅛" x 3" (5 x 7.6cm)

- Key fob hardware: 1½" (3.8cm) diameter ring and ⁵⁄₁₆" (0.8cm) rivet

- Rivet setter for a ⁵⁄₁₆" (0.8cm) rivet

- Key Fob pattern (page 126)

- Color in your preferred medium (optional)

- Edge burnisher and gum tragacanth or mink oil paste

- Your preferred finish

- Pyrography burner

- Small writer and small shader pen tips

- Unwaxed graphite paper

- Non-slip shelving liner

- White rubber/plastic eraser or artist kneaded eraser

- Razor blade

- Tape

- Painter's tape

- Pen

- Scissors

1 **Prepare.** Make a copy of the Key Fob pattern on page 126. Tape a piece of non-slip shelving liner to your table. Place a dry vegetable-tanned key fob cutout close to the top edge of the liner with the grain (smooth) side up.

Transfer the pattern. Position the pattern over the key fob and tape one side of the pattern to the table in two places with painter's tape. Place unwaxed graphite paper between the pattern and the leather with the graphite side down. Trace the pattern onto the dry leather.

Burn the stems, leaves, and berries. Following the pattern lines, burn the stems and leaves using a small writer (or skew pen if desired). Avoid pressing hard while burning because it makes the lines wider, filling in the leaves. Burn the berries using the point of a writer pen.

Burn the rabbit. Continue to burn the rabbit that you transferred from the pattern using the small writer pen.

Add shading to stems and leaves. Using a small shader pen, add some light shading to the stems and leaves. Use the same technique described for the coaster project (step 5 on page 62).

6

Add shading to the rabbit. Using the same shader pen, add shading to the rabbit while referring to the pattern. Turn your project so that the shader is on the inside of the shape with the toe of the shader on the inside edge of the line. If you are having difficulty with the shader pen, you can also shade using a stippling or scribbling technique as described in the "Different Types of Shading" sidebar on page 39.

7

Clean up. Erase all of the transfer lines. Use the edge of a razor blade to lightly scrape any edges that are bumpy and any dark splotches in the shading.

Add color (optional). If you wish, add color to your project. Test your color on a scrap piece of leather. I used an acrylic wash of olive green on the leaves and a pink marker over the berries.

Add finish. Once your color is dry, you can finish the edges of your cutout using an edge burnisher as described on the coaster project (step 9 on page 63). After testing the effects of your finish over your color, apply the finish to your project.

Assemble. Bend the key fob tab over the key ring and attach the rivet by inserting the rivet piece with the long post through the backside of the key fob. Attach the rivet cap to the long post that is showing through the frontside of the leather, and then seal them together using a rivet setter.

Bookmark

Level: Beginner

Bookmarks are fun to create and easy to personalize. You can purchase bookmark cutouts, ready to burn, or you can cut them from a piece of leather. I recommend using leather in the 4 to 6 oz. range if you cut your own. You can also punch a hole in the end of the bookmark if you want to add leather lace and embellishments.

Materials and Tools

- Vegetable-tanned leather bookmark, approx. 1½" x 8" (3.8 x 20cm)
- Bookmark pattern (page 126)
- Color in your preferred medium (optional)
- Edge burnisher and gum tragacanth or mink oil paste
- Your preferred finish
- Pyrography burner
- Small writer and small shader pen tips
- Unwaxed graphite paper
- Non-slip shelving liner
- White rubber/plastic eraser or artist kneaded eraser
- Razor blade
- Tape
- Painter's tape
- Pen
- Scissors
- Optional for embellishments:
    - ⅛" (0.3cm) leather hole punch
    - Leather lace, ⅛" x 13" (0.3 x 33cm)
    - Large-hole bead

because, officially, the principal ... and nothing else ... he'd seen ... coach's office in the ... house last ... and there were so many rumors ... who'd been there didn't know what

... they'd all come back, Cully's eyes had a ... hunched over. Trace and Brad walked ... a swath in the crowd—a tic in Trace's ... Brad's face so empty it seemed comical ... they didn't blame them for being ... a girl was a girl. But, Dex said ... he passed one of the three ... hello.

... and another girl he ... loudly, and as he ... This is all just a setup. Br... They don't have to for...

... WERE DRIV... ...tion...

They we... but Week... droma...

... He hadn't been with a girl ... community center for a teen ... ened to be trying to make ... with the dial of the radio ... a real sound system in this ... There was a huge red zit ... ing in a cartoon. "Let me ask ...

The post-work traffic ... another, driving, looking ... "I don't know." He ... "After all that ...

... party over as ... at the Dairy Que... early for that ... ing her hair or ... you think she likes you ... were there any other ...

Quaker ... ere one of ... slackly when ... lady wanted full

...es," Weeks told ... and sometimes th... made him stupid ... stupid to begin with

1 **Prepare.** Make a copy of the Bookmark pattern on page 126. If you want to add a name to the bookmark, print the name from your computer in the exact size you want to use that will fit the pattern. Tape the name in position on the pattern and make a copy so you can use it as a pattern without the layers of tape and paper.

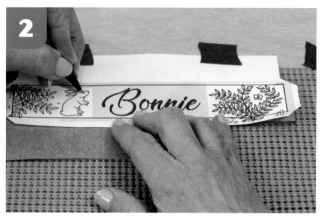

2

Transfer the pattern. Position the pattern over the bookmark and tape one side of the pattern to the table in two places with painter's tape. Cut notches in the pattern at the corners so you can line up the pattern on the bookmark. Place unwaxed graphite paper between the pattern and the leather with the graphite side down. Trace the pattern onto the dry leather.

3

Burn the stems, leaves, and berries. Following the pattern lines, burn the stems and leaves using a small writer (or skew pen if desired). Avoid pressing hard while burning because it makes the lines wider, filling in the leaves. Burn the berries using the point of a writer pen.

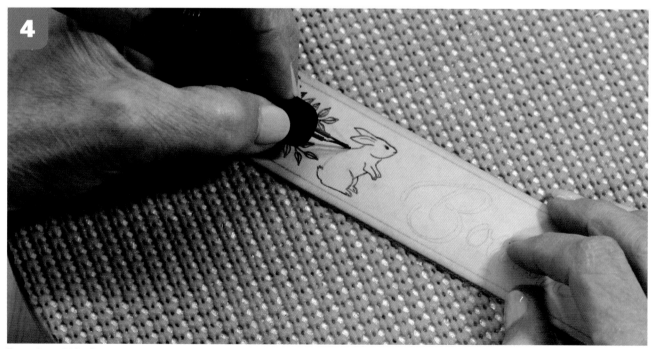

4

Burn the rabbit. Continue to burn the rabbit that you transferred from the pattern using the small writer pen.

5

Outline and fill in the letters (optional). If your bookmark has a name in the design, use a small writer pen to outline the lettering and then fill in the letters with the writer. If the leather pulls when filling in the letters and shows white cracks from the leather underneath, use the writer to dab the surface of the leather to even out the burn color.

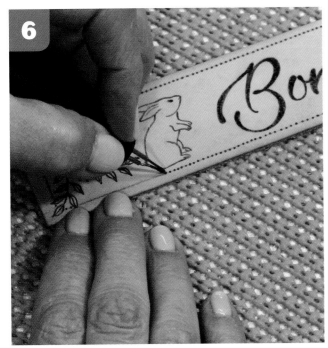

6

Add a border (optional). If you want to add a border like this example to your bookmark, follow the transferred border line with little dots using your writer pen.

7

Add shading to stems and leaves. Using a small shader pen, add some light shading to the stems and leaves. Use the same technique described for the coaster project (page 62).

Bookmark

Add shading to rabbit. Using the same shader pen, add shading to the rabbit while referring to the pattern. Turn your project so that the shader is on the inside of the shape with the toe of the shader on the inside edge of the line. If you are having difficulty with the shader pen, you can also shade using a stippling or scribbling technique as described in the "Different Types of Shading" sidebar on page 39.

Clean up. Erase all of the transfer lines. Use the edge of a razor blade to lightly scrape any edges that are bumpy and any dark splotches in the shading.

10

Add color (optional). If you wish, add color to your project. Test your color on a scrap piece of leather. I used an acrylic wash of olive green on the leaves and a pink marker over the berries.

11

Add finish. Once your color is dry, you can finish the edges of your cutout using an edge burnisher as described on the coaster project (step 9 on page 63). After testing the effects of your finish over your color, apply the finish to your project.

12

Embellish (optional). On the example project, I embellished the bookmark by adding a bead and leather tassel. First, I cut a hole in the bookmark using a ⅛" (0.3cm) leather hole punch. I then cut a 13" (33cm) piece of leather suede lace (⅛" [0.3cm] wide) and folded it in half to form a loop. I threaded the lace loop through the hole and then pulled the loose ends of the lace through the loop. I threaded the lace ends through a large-hole bead and tied an overhand knot.

Journal Cover

Level: Intermediate

Planners and journals feel more important and expensive when they are covered in leather. You can personalize your planner or journal cover with pyrography. In this project, we will concentrate on the use of the writer, skew, and shader pens. Leathercrafters can add their own touches to their projects, such as leather tooling or stitching the edges, but do the tooling before the burning and make sure the leather is completely dry before transferring and burning the designs.

Note: Test the gears pattern on a scrap piece of leather. If you are having difficulty with the small shapes, you can enlarge the pattern parts and position them within the template before you transfer it onto your project.

Materials and Tools

- Vegetable-tanned leather, 4 oz., enough to wrap around your journal with a flap, plus an additional 6" (15.5cm) for inside pockets
- A planner/journal (I used one with a coiled binding)
- Steampunk Cover patterns (pages 116, 117, and 118)
- Sharp utility knife or heavy-duty rotary cutter
- Metal ruler
- Cutting mat
- Permanent leather glue (such as Leather Weld or contact cement)
- Eyelet setter and 3 eyelets, ¼" (0.6cm)
- Leather hole punch, ⁵⁄₃₂" (0.4cm)
- Heavy, flat object (I used my tooling granite slab)
- Concho and screw back
- Leather calf lace, ³⁄₃₂" (0.25cm) wide, one 13" (33cm) and three 40" (102cm) strands

- Color in your preferred medium (optional, not used on the example)
- Edge burnisher and gum tragacanth or mink oil paste
- Your preferred finish
- Pyrography burner
- Small writer, medium or small skew, and small shader pen tips
- Small circle pen tips (optional)
- Unwaxed graphite paper
- Non-slip shelving liner
- White rubber/plastic eraser or artist kneaded eraser
- Razor blade
- Tape
- Painter's tape
- Pencil
- Scissors

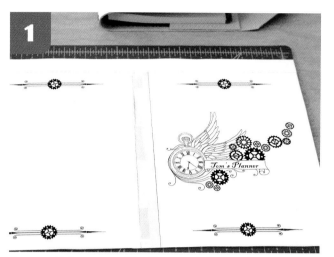

1 Prepare. Make a copy of the Steampunk Cover patterns on pages 116, 117, and 118, adjusting the size for your planner or journal if necessary. Tape together the flap, back cover, and front cover patterns, leaving the gray bars for the thickness of the journal.

2 Cut the cover leather and pockets. Open your planner or journal and place it on the flesh (rough) side of the leather. Position the journal to avoid blemishes and leave plenty of additional leather for the flap. Cut the leather, using a sharp utility knife or heavy-duty rotary cutter, into a long rectangular shape, adding an additional ⅜" (1cm) at the top and the bottom of the journal. Also cut two inside pockets, both 3" (7.6cm) wide and the same height as the cover you just cut.

3 Mark the front cover pocket. Position the journal front cover so that it is centered top to bottom on the leather, which should leave a ⅜" (1cm) leather margin. Position the left edge so that it has the same margin allowance as the top and bottom margin allowances. Trace around the top, bottom, and left side of the actual journal cover with a pencil. To finish marking the front inside pocket placement, place a mark 3" (7.6cm) from the left pencil line on the top and bottom lines. Align the front cover pattern in place (double check its position) and mark the hole for the concho through the pattern onto the leather. Punch a hole for the concho using a ⁵⁄₃₂" (0.4cm) leather hole punch. Do not add the concho until later.

Tip:

When tracing around the journal cover to mark the pocket placement, you only need to go about 3" (7.6cm) over on the top and bottom to avoid leaving a pencil line inside the final project.

Glue the front cover pocket. Apply a permanent leather adhesive to the top 3" (7.6cm), bottom 3" (7.6cm), and left leather margins that you marked with the pencil. Do not put glue on the pencil line, just close to it. Position and glue the front inside pocket into place. Put a heavy, flat object, such as your tooling granite slab, on the pocket and allow the glue to dry.

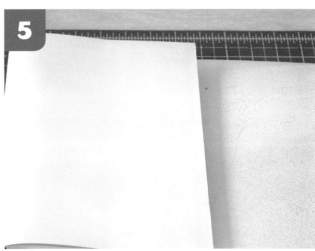

Position the front and back cover. After the glue dries, slip the front journal cover into the front leather pocket you just created. Fold the journal and position the front and back journal cover so that their outside edges align.

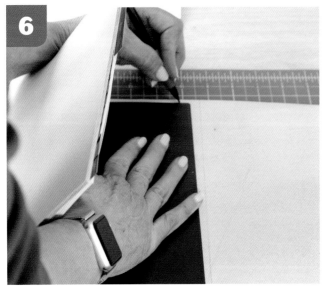

Mark and glue the back cover pocket. To mark the back inside cover margin, place a vertical pencil line ⅜" (1cm) to the right of the journal cover. Holding the back journal cover in place, lift the front cover and journal pages out of the way and trace the top, bottom, and right edge of the actual journal back cover with a pencil, giving you a ⅜" (1cm) margin around the back cover. To finish marking the back inside pocket placement, place a mark 3" (7.6cm) from the right pencil line on the top and bottom lines. Remove the journal from the front inside pocket. Glue the back inside pocket in place, applying the glue as you did on the front cover (close to the pencil line but not touching). Put a heavy weight on the pocket and allow it to dry.

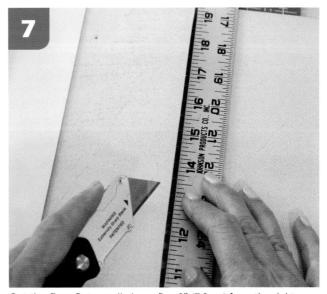

Cut the flap. Cut a preliminary flap 3" (7.6cm) from the right edge of the glued back inside pocket. Slip the journal back into the front and back inside pockets. Fold the journal closed. Check the pattern sizing by aligning the pattern on the front cover and wrapping it around to the back cover. Fold the flap's pattern and leather onto the front. Observe the placement of the top and bottom pattern designs on the front cover and back cover. Are they approximately centered horizontally on the cover or do they need to be adjusted? Is the flap overlapping the cover too far? Adjust the pattern as necessary. Recheck the placement. Once you have it placed as desired, mark where to trim the front flap. Trim the flap corners to match the gray triangles in the pattern.

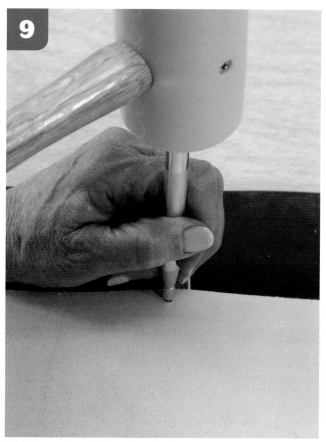

Punch the eyelet and concho holes. With the journal in the leather cover and positioned so the top and bottom cover are folded closed and in alignment, mark the top and bottom spine on the inside of the cover on the center mark. Remove the journal from the cover. Check the pencil marks for center alignment on the spine. Mark ¼" (0.6cm) from the outside edge on the top and bottom center spine for how far in to place the eyelet hole. Next mark the flap eyelet hole placement. It should be placed halfway down the outside edge and ¼" (0.6cm) in from the edge. Using a ⁵⁄₃₂" (0.4cm) leather hole punch, punch the three holes.

Add the eyelets. Using a rivet/eyelet setter, place a ¼" (0.6cm) eyelet through the front of the leather with the widest part of the eyelet on the grain side. Place the eyelet in the indentation in the base of the setter, both the widest part of the eyelet and the grain side down. Place the eyelet punch on the top of the eyelet and hammer the punch until the eyelet is flat and holding the leather from both sides of the hole.

Tip:

If you have never set an eyelet before, practice on a scrap piece of your leather.

Tip:

When I am transferring a detailed, precise pattern, I use a mechanical pencil instead of a red pen because the lines are thinner. It's harder to see where you've been with a pencil, but I pay attention, working in a methodical manner over the pattern. I also check the transfer very well for omissions before I remove the pattern.

Transfer the pattern. Position the pattern over the cover and tape one side of the pattern to the table in two places. Place unwaxed graphite paper between the pattern and the leather with the graphite side down, securing them to the table with painter's tape. Trace the pattern onto the dry leather. Use a ruler to transfer the straight lines.

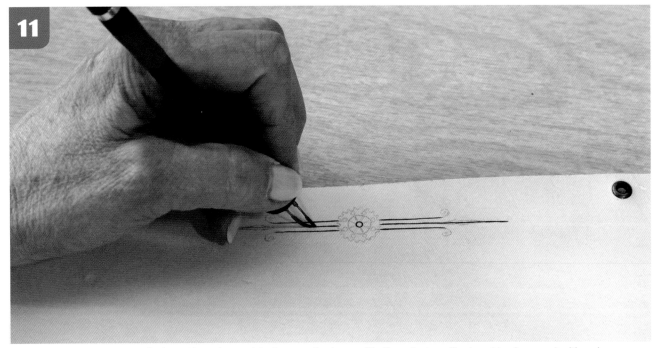

Burn the lines on the gear designs. Burn the straight lines on the top and bottom designs (front and back covers) with a skew pen. Burn the curved ends of the lines with a small writer pen. I used a 0.8mm (⅟₃₂") ball writer. Avoid pressing hard while burning with the writer so the curved ends blend in with the skew lines. I used small circle pens (0.071"/1.8mm and 0.100"/2.5mm) to burn the circles on the gears throughout the cover designs. Using circle branders gives you quick precision, but this is optional, as you can also use a writer pen to draw the circles.

Burn the banner and clockface. Using a skew pen, burn the banner and then the clockface. Use the skew pen to burn the curvy lines around the clock and use the small writer pen to add the curls on the ends of the lines.

Burn the wings. Using a skew pen, burn the straight and curved lines on the wings. Use a writer pen to burn the sharp curves on the tips of the wing feathers.

Burn the journal name. Using a small writer pen, burn the name of your planner or journal. If you want to personalize the name, type the text on your computer and print it out in the correct size to transfer. I used an old vintage handwritten text called "Blackadder ITC" for this project.

Burn the gears. Using a small writer pen, outline the gears. I used a 0.8mm (1/32") ball writer. For the smallest gears, when I outlined the outer circles, I used the writer pen to start at the outline and push outward to create the cogs in the gears. For the medium to large gears, I created a double circle for the outside band on the gear and filled it in with the writer to create a thick band. I then added an outer band of dashes for the ends of the cogs. Next, I created a "U" shape, connecting the dash to the outer band of the cog and back to the next dash. I then filled in the rest of the gear with the writer pen.

16

Add the shading. Using a small round-toe shader, shade the outer rim of the clockface. Add some light shading to the inside clockface. Add light shading to the banner, following the pattern. Add shading to the wings, following the pattern. The shading will be a little darker at the base of each feather and on the feathers on the back wing where it intersects with the front wing. Start your shading where it is darkest and drag then lift where it starts to fade.

17

Clean up. Erase all of the transfer lines. Use the edge of a razor blade to lightly scrape any edges that are bumpy and any dark splotches in the shading. See the section "Touching Up Mistakes" on page 47.

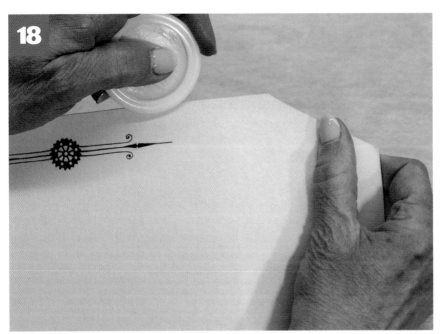

18

Burnish the edges. Finish the edges of your journal cover by wetting them or applying gum tragacanth or mink oil paste, making sure you do not get any of it on the front or back of the cover. Then use an edge burnisher on the edge by rubbing the burnisher back and forth until it is smooth.

Tip:

If you want to add color to your project, add the color medium of your choice before you apply the finish. You can choose from any of the color mediums in the "Adding Color to Pyrography" section on page 50. Test all the colors you are going to use on a scrap piece of leather. After testing the colors on your leather, test the effects of your finish over your color.

19

Add finish. Apply the finish of your choice to your project to protect the leather. My finish of preference for journal covers is Fiebing's brand Saddle Lac. It is a spray that changes the leather to a vintage amber color and hardens the surface to protect it from daily wear.

Tip:

Conchos come in many designs. I used a gear concho to complement the theme of the steampunk design. If you do not want to use a concho, you can make the lace strands of the flap long enough to wrap around the cover and tie off with themselves.

20

Add the concho. Add the concho to the hole in the front cover by placing the screw post through the front and then placing the screw back on the inside under the flap. Tighten the screw back. When placing the journal back into the inside front pocket, you'll need to lift the concho to slip the journal into the pocket so it doesn't get caught on the concho screw back.

21

Add the flap tie. Cut a piece of leather calf lace approximately 13" (33cm) long. Fold it in half and feed the loop through the flap eyelet hole. Thread the ends of the lace through the loop and tighten the loop by working it smaller as you pull on the lace ends. Trim the ends of the lace even.

22

Add the cover binding. Cut three pieces of leather calf lace approximately 40" (102cm) long each. Stack the ends so they all have the finished side on top. Thread them through the cover spine top eyelet hole (from the outside of the cover to the inside). Pull them through the eyelet until you have about 4" (10cm) of lace on the inside. Wrap a piece of painter's tape around the three pieces so they do not slide back through the eyelet hole. Start braiding the three strands evenly, keeping the finished side of the lace on top. Braid the strands until you have enough length to meet the eyelet hole at the bottom of the outside cover spine. Wrap painter's tape around the end of the braid before it would go through the bottom eyelet hole to hold the braid's tension until you can feed the long strands through the hole.

23

Finish the cover binding and bookmarks. Feed the lace strands through the cover spine bottom eyelet hole (from the outside of the cover to the inside). Because the strands are so long, you may need to feed them through the eyelet separately. Keep the finished side of the lace in the same direction as you feed the strands through the hole. Insert the journal into the leather cover, and then feed each strand up through the wire coil. If your planner or journal does not have a coil, bring your lace up through the center of the book. Once through the coils, straighten the lace strands. Remove the painter's tape from the start of the strands, and then gather and tie them in an overhand knot with the shorter strands at the top eyelet, pulling tight. Work the lace to tighten the overhand knot as much as possible. Tuck the short beginning lace ends into the coil to hide them. Take the long lace strands and pull them down through the book. Trim them to the length you desire to use as bookmarks. I trimmed mine to hang out the bottom of the journal about 2" (5cm), which makes it easy to use them to open to the bookmarked page.

Tip:

Feed the lace through the journal coil by holding the journal so the coil is vertical/perpendicular to the table with the bottom of the journal at the highest point. Send each strand through separately by turning the strand so it curves toward the journal pages. This will stop the strands from trying to slide out between the coils, because they will be pressing against the compressed journal pages.

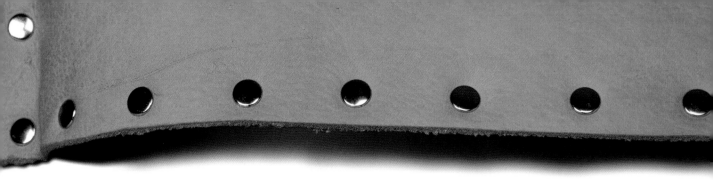

Fringed Pillow

Level: Advanced

This project is considered advanced pyrography because it is almost entirely rendered using a shader pen. The shader is the most difficult of the pen categories to master because it takes practice to learn the pen angle, heat setting, and speed required in order to achieve flat shading tones without a lot of unintended blobs.

Test shading a small section of the horse on a scrap piece of leather. If you have not mastered the shader pen but still wish to create this project, you can burn the horse using a stippling or scribbling method as described in the "Different Types of Shading" sidebar on page 39.

This particular project utilizes milled vegetable-tanned leather, which means the leather has been tumbled during the tanning process in order to make it very soft. While milled leather is not the best for tooling/stamping, it is great for pyrography.

Materials and Tools

- Milled vegetable-tanned shoulder leather, 3 to 4 oz.,18" x 25" (46 x 64cm) or two 18" x 13" (46 x 33cm) pieces, plus two 6" x 12" (15.5 x 31cm) pieces for the fringe
- Polyester fiberfill batting
- Running Horse patterns (pages 119 and 122)
- Sharp utility knife or heavy-duty rotary cutter
- Cutting mat
- Metal ruler
- Edge burnisher and gum tragacanth or mink oil paste
- Your preferred finish
- Permanent leather glue (such as Leather Weld or contact cement)
- 2x4 (50x100mm) board
- Rivet setter and 40 small rivets, ¼" (0.6cm) (56 rivets if using two pieces of leather for the body of the pillow)
- Leather hole punch, ⅛" (0.3cm)
- Metal fringe cutting template and a rotary wheel cutter, or sharp sewing scissors
- Pyrography burner
- Small and medium writer and shader pen tips
- Unwaxed graphite paper
- Artist kneaded eraser
- Razor blade
- Painter's tape
- Red pen
- Scissors
- Paper binder clips

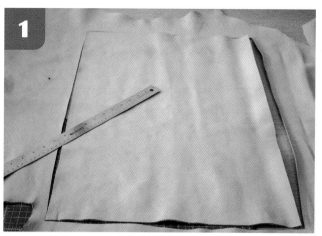

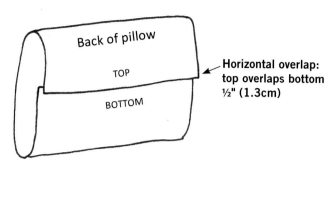

Pillow Diagram 1

Prepare. Make a copy of the Running Horse patterns on pages 119 and 122. Cut the leather pillow body using a sharp utility knife or heavy-duty rotary cutter, cutting mat, and metal ruler. Fold it according to the diagram (Pillow Diagram 1). Overlap the top and bottom flaps by ½" (1.3cm). Transfer the rivet pattern only on the horizontal overlap by burning a dot with a small writer pen through the paper pattern in the center of each circle. Note: If you cannot cut the 18" x 25" (46 x 64cm) pillow body out of your piece of leather, cut two 18" x 13" (46 x 33cm) pieces, which will require you to add rivets to the top and bottom of the pillow when putting it together instead of riveting a horizontal overlap.

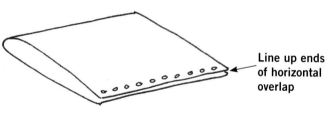

Pillow Diagram 2

Punch the horizontal rivet holes. Use a ⅛" (0.3cm) leather hole punch to make the holes on the top horizontal flap where you burned the mark for the rivet placement. When you finish the row, fold the leather in half so the two ends align (Pillow Diagram 2). Punch through each hole to create a matching hole on the opposite end of the leather.

Tip:

Unlike regular vegetable-tanned leather, milled vegetable-tanned leather causes the transferred graphite lines to smear when erasing with a white plastic/rubber eraser. An artist kneaded eraser works best to remove the graphite on milled leather. If you do not have a kneaded eraser, you can use a piece of painter's tape to stick on the leather and then quickly pull up the tape to lift off the graphite. You will need to repeat this until you remove all the smudges and lighten any dark transfer lines. After the piece of tape picks up enough graphite, it will need to be replaced with a fresh piece of tape.

Transfer the horse pattern. Refold the leather so that the grain (smooth) side is on the outside and the top overlaps the bottom across the back of the pillow (to match Pillow Diagram 1). Adjust the horizontal overlap position so that the end rivet holes will align with one of the rivet holes that will be placed down the side. On my project, I made the horizontal overlap on the back of the pillow higher than the center line in order to hide a blemish on the leather. If I had placed the overlapping line in the center, the blemish would have been on the front of the pillow. By moving the horizontal overlap higher on the back of the pillow, it rolled the blemish to the bottom of the pillow, where it would be hidden. Once you have the horizontal overlapping line positioned, carefully hold and flip the leather over without losing the alignment. You can use paper binder clips to hold the sides together as you flip. The front will now be on top and in position for the pattern to be placed. Place the pattern in the center and tape it in two places on the top with painter's tape. Slip a piece of graphite paper under the pattern with the graphite side down on the leather. Trace the main lines of the pattern using a red pen to see where you transferred. After transferring a few lines, lift the pattern to check whether the transfer is showing on the leather or backside of the pattern. Also check how light or dark the transferred lines appear and adjust your pressure accordingly.

Burn the horse reference lines. After transferring the pattern, unfold the leather so you can burn the horse on one single thickness of leather. Since graphite smears easily on milled leather, I chose to very lightly burn the main transfer lines of the horse using a very small writer pen (a 0.8mm [1/32"] ball writer). Burn the lines light enough so that when you shade next to the line, the line will seem to disappear. After you have the main lines burned, erase the graphite using a kneaded eraser or tape pick-up (see tip on page 90).

Fringed Pillow

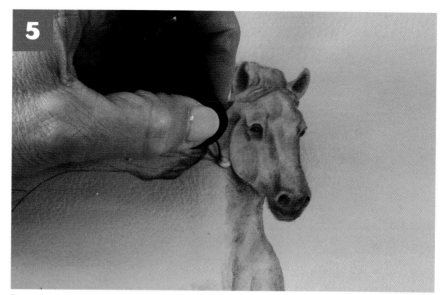

5

Burn the horse. Burn the eyes and outlines of the ears and nostrils using a small writer pen. Use a small round-toe shader pen to darken in the ears and inside of the nostrils. To shade in small spaces, tip the pen into a more vertical position and use the toe of the tip. To shade the horse, start at the outer edges of the shape and pull toward the inside of the shape to fade the stroke.

6

Burn the mane and tail. Using a small round-toe shader pen, shade the main colors (or tones) of the mane and tail, following the pattern. Start the shading next to the horse and move in the direction the hair is flowing away from the horse. Use a medium writer pen to burn the hair lines on the mane and tail, trailing off of the background shading in random lines.

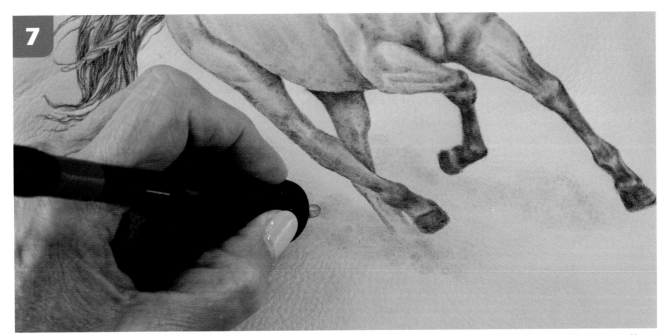

7

Burn the dust cloud. Use the small round-toe shader pen to create dust clouds under the horse's hooves, following the pattern. Keep the temperature low so the dust burns light, using a circular and curved motion like shading an arc over the top of an O.

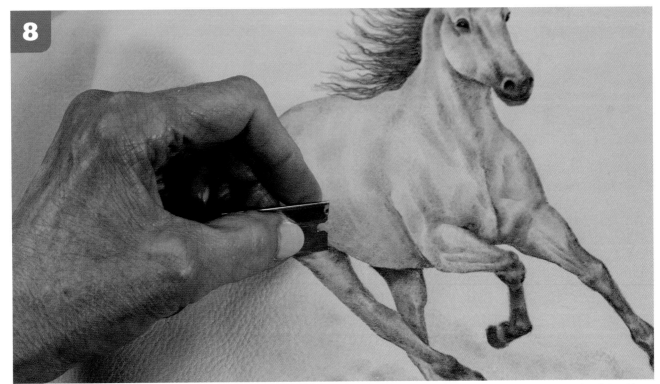

8

Clean up. Use a razor blade to touch up any edges that are bumpy and any dark splotches in the shading. See the section "Touching Up Mistakes" on page 47.

Add finish. After you complete the burning, finish the edges of your leather pieces. Carefully apply a product such as gum tragacanth or mink oil paste to smooth down all the leather edges, making sure you do not get any of it on the front of the leather. Apply the finishing product of your choice to the grain side of all the leather. After the grain side is dry, apply the gum tragacanth or mink oil paste to the back/flesh side of the fringe pieces and burnish down the nap so it is smoother. This will help keep the milled leather from shedding after the pillow is completed.

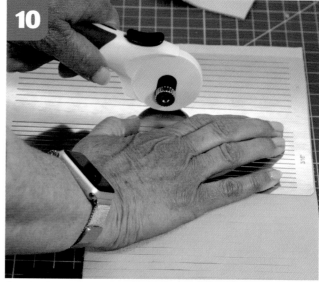

Cut the fringe. After the backs of the fringe pieces are dry, cut the fringe panels with parallel lines, ¼" (0.6cm) wide, leaving a ½" to ⅝" (1.3 to 1.6cm) uncut border down one long edge. I used a metal fringe-cutting template and a rotary wheel cutter. You can also mark ¼" (0.6cm) lines using a ruler and cut the fringe using sharp sewing scissors.

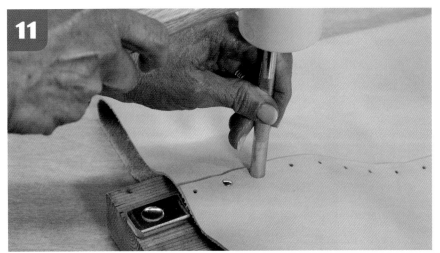

11

Tip:

Once you snap the rivet cap onto its base, the rivet is held together. You can add the bottom and cap of several rivets in a row before setting them with the rivet setter.

Add the first row of rivets. Fold the pillow leather with the grain side on the outside and overlapping the top and bottom edges on the backside of the pillow. The top flap should sit on top of the bottom flap. Spread a permanent leather adhesive, such as Leather Weld or contact cement, between the rivet holes on the bottom flap. Glue the top and bottom flaps in place, making sure all the holes align. Then, starting with the second hole in from one edge, add the rivets until you reach the next-to-last hole on the far edge. Leave the two end holes unriveted. They will be done when the sides are riveted. To add the rivets, thread a rivet bottom, which has a long post, from the inside of the pillow through the bottom flap hole, then the top flap hole. Snap a rivet cap onto the top of the rivet bottom post. Place the rivet bottom onto the rivet setter base in the indentation designed to hold the rivet in place. Place the domed end of the rivet setter rod over the rivet cap to strike the rod with a leather mallet. I used a piece of a 2x4 (50x100mm) board under the rivet setter base because my poundo board was too large to fit into the pillow, and I wanted to protect the burned image of the horse on the opposite side.

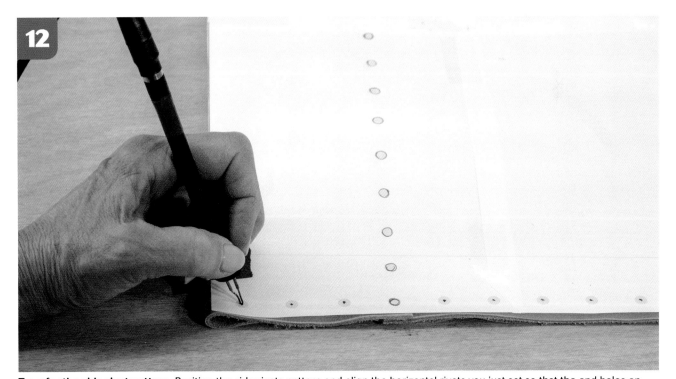

12

Transfer the side rivet pattern. Position the side rivets pattern and align the horizontal rivets you just set so that the end holes on that row align with the same side rivet holes you chose in step 3. Transfer the side rivet pattern by burning through the pattern with the small writer pen.

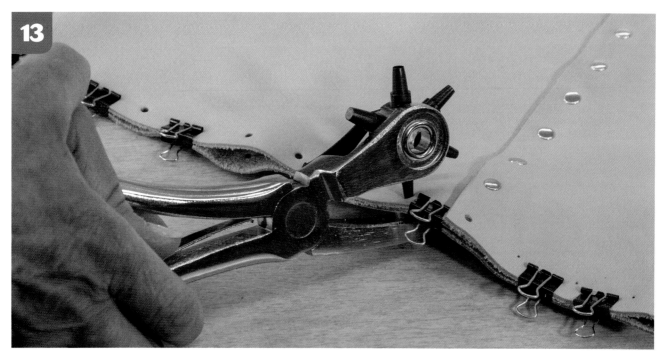

Punch the side rivet holes. Use paper binder clips to help hold the front and back leather pieces in place while punching the holes through the sides. Punch through the front and back layers at the same time.

Burn the rivet placement on the fringe. Line up the side rivet pattern with the outside edge of the fringe on the grain side where you left the small uncut margin. Burn the rivet placement on the fringe pieces by burning through the pattern with the small writer pen. Punch holes on the fringe where the burn marks for the rivets are indicated.

Tip:

When the pillow is stuffed, setting the last rows of rivets is easier if you place the rivet setter base on a piece of a 2x4 (50x100mm) board, lifting the base up to the height of the rivet.

Attach one side of the fringe to the pillow. Add rivets to one side by threading a rivet post up through the back of the pillow, then through the back of the fringe, and finally through the front of the pillow. The grain side of the fringe should be facing toward the front of the pillow. Snap the rivet cap onto the post and use the rivet setter and hammer to add the rivets down one side of the pillow.

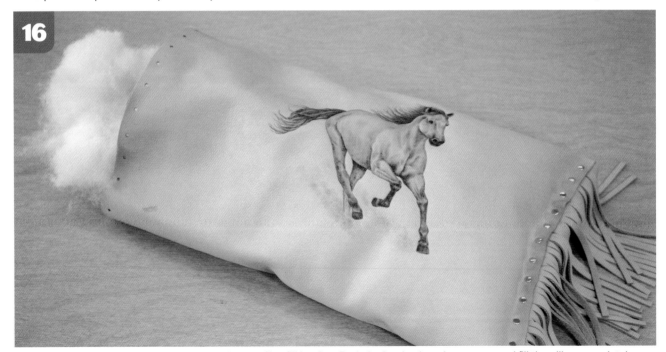

Finish the pillow. Stuff the pillow with the polyester fiberfill batting. Pack the batting into the corners and fill the pillow completely except for the last couple of inches (last few centimeters). Add the fringe and rivets to the remaining side, starting with one corner. After you set about three rivets, stuff that corner with batting. Keep setting rivets and stuffing the pillow under the finished rivets. When you have three rivets left to set, finish stuffing the batting and hand-set the rivets. Set the final three rivets using the rivet setter base and rod.

Fringed Pillow

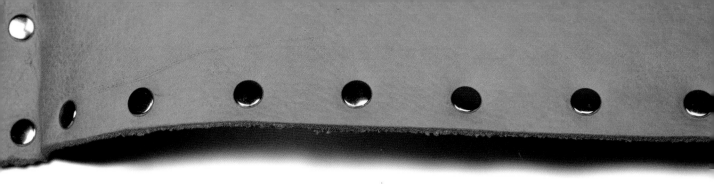

3D Quail

Level: Advanced

The project in this chapter will give you experience burning on a rounded, 3D surface. Burning on a rounded surface is more challenging than burning on a flat one because you have to change the pen angle as you move across the surface. Review the section "Working on a 3D Surface" on page 43. Since the purpose of this project is to experience burning on a 3D surface—and not to learn how to model a 3D leather project—I kept the project simple and concentrated on making only the quail head, body, and tail three-dimensional. The feet and log are flat and part of the background. If you are a leatherworker and have modeling experience, you can make the entire picture three-dimensional.

Materials and Tools

- Vegetable-tanned calfskin leather, 2 to 3 oz., large enough to fit in your picture frame plus an additional 1½" (3.8cm) on all sides

- Quail patterns (pages 119 and 120)

- Rustic picture frame (I used a 10" x 10" [25.5 x 25.5cm] frame)

- Plywood to fit the frame, approx. ⅛" (0.3cm) thick (I used birch plywood)

- Plastic bucket or tub (large enough to soak your leather piece)

- Oven-bake modeling clay (such as Sculpey®)

- Baking sheet, aluminum foil, and oven (to bake clay)

- Weighted flat objects (I used two paper-filled binders)

- Leather modeling tools: spoon-shaped and sharp

- Permanent leather glue (such as Leather Weld or contact cement)

- Rivet setter and 44 small rivets, ¼" (0.6cm)

- Leather hole punch, ⅛" (0.3cm)

- Drill with ⅛" (0.3cm) bit

- Your preferred finish

- Polyester fiberfill batting

- Pyrography burner

- Small and medium writer, small round-toe shader, and thin round-heeled skew pen tips

- Unwaxed graphite paper

- Non-slip shelving liner, approx. 1 sq. ft. (930 sq. cm)

- White rubber/plastic eraser or artist kneaded eraser

- Razor blade

- Painter's tape

- Pen

- Scissors

- Metal ruler

- Utility knife

- Cutting board

1 **Prepare.** There are four things to do to prepare for this project. First, make two copies of the Quail pattern on page 120 in a size to fit in your picture frame. Second, cut the plywood to fit into your picture frame as the backer behind the picture. It will be larger than the portion of the picture that shows when the frame is hung. Test that your plywood fits into the frame. Third, make a copy of the Quail rivets pattern on page 119 in a size to fit the measurements of the interior frame opening that the picture will show through. If you need to adjust the length of the sides to make a rectangle, make an extra copy of the pattern and then cut and tape the pattern to fit your frame. You can also make your rivet pattern with a ruler and mark a paper template of your own. Fourth, cut a piece of leather calf skin about 1 ½" (3.8cm) larger than the plywood you cut.

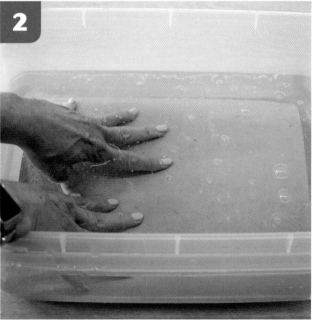

Wet the leather. Thoroughly wet the leather by placing it in a plastic bucket or tub of clear water and holding it underwater until bubbles stop forming. When removing the leather, shake off the excess water and then place it on a very flat, non-porous surface, such as a granite tooling slab or countertop. Smooth the leather flat and allow it to absorb the water and start the drying process. After a couple of hours, check to see if the surface is still wet when you lift a corner. When the leather is ready to mold, it should still be dark in color, very cool and moist, but not visibly wet or leave water visible on the table when you lift the corner.

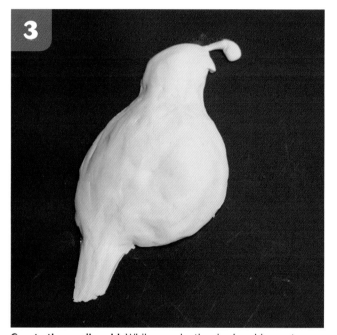

Create the quail mold. While your leather is absorbing water, place one of the quail patterns on a baking sheet. You can place a protective sheet (silicon baking sheet, piece of aluminum foil, or parchment paper) under the pattern. Build the clay model on top of the pattern using a hardening clay such as Sculpey. Sculpey recommends adding a crumpled aluminum foil filler to the core of your model if it will be over ½" (1.3cm) thick. I added a small oval pad of crushed aluminum foil to the inside of the bird body shape before adding clay over it. Add clay by tearing off a chunk of clay, kneading it until it is soft and pliable, and then pressing it onto the pattern within the body shape. Cover the aluminum foil padding and the entire inside shape of the bird pattern (head, head plume, body, and tail). Build the mold so it is higher in the middle and tapers down to the paper on the edges. Once you create the form of the bird, smooth the clay surface to get rid of lumps. Bake the clay in your oven according to the package directions. After the clay is baked, let the clay mold cool.

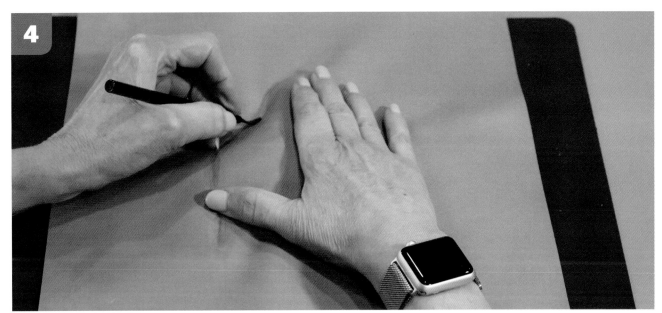

Shape the leather over the mold. When the mold is cool and the leather is ready, position the leather over the mold. Start shaping and stretching the leather. Beginning at the highest point on the mold, gradually stretch the leather by pushing down both sides of the mold with your hands. Repeat this process down all sides of the mold. After the leather is stretched a little, hold the leather in place on the top of the mold with one hand while using a modeling spoon tool to press the edge around the mold where it meets the table.

Crease and finish shaping the leather. Repeat this process using a sharp modeling tool to crease the edge where the mold meets the table. Let the leather dry. You may need to add some weighted flat objects to get the leather surrounding the quail to lay flat. I used three-ring binders filled with papers. Check to see that you didn't get a wrinkle in the leather under the books or weights. If you do have a wrinkle forming, add some water on your finger and smooth it out. Then add the weighted object while pulling the leather straight.

3D Quail

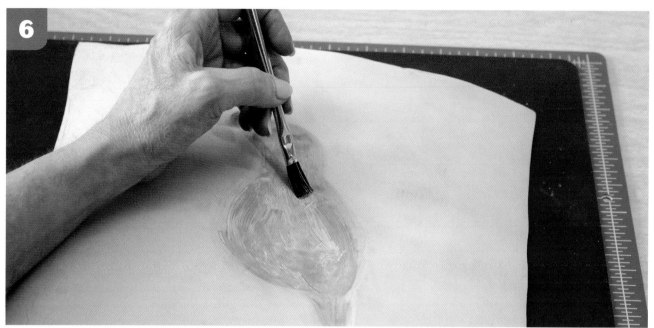

Stabilize the molded leather. When the leather is dry, brush glue on the backside (flesh side of the leather) of the bird where the leather is molded. I used Leather Weld because it dries quickly but stays tacky. Next glue the leather to the plywood board. Start by spreading glue on one half of the leather, from the edge of the side up to the edge of the bird molding. Press the glued leather onto the plywood board in position. Lay weighted objects on the glued leather that are flat on the bottom and will not mar the leather.

Add batting. After the glue is dry, lift the unglued side and add a little polyester fiber batting under the bird molding, enough to fill the void but not totally stuff it. Glue the remaining leather to the plywood board. Add weighted objects until the glue is dry.

8

Trim the leather to fit. After the glue is dry, trim the excess leather from the plywood board. In order to not damage the molded bird while trimming the leather, I placed a couple of thick hardcover books under the cutting board and allowed the molded bird to hang off the edge. Cut the leather on the cutting board using a metal ruler and a sharp utility knife.

9

Tip:

Sometimes tape can mar the surface of the leather. Test your tape on the leather or cut your pattern so that the paper can hang off one edge to be taped to the table or around to the back of the plywood.

Mark the rivet holes. On my project, the leather will be attached to the front of the frame, so the rivets will be placed along the edge of the leather. If you are mounting your project from behind the frame like a standard picture, your rivets will be placed along the inside edge of the interior frame opening where the picture shows through. Trim the Quail rivets pattern (or your own template pattern) to the appropriate rivet placement, either along the edge of the leather or along the inside frame opening. Once the pattern is in position, tape it with painter's tape. Check the placement of the rivets with your frame. Using a small writer pen, burn a dot through the paper onto the leather in the center of each rivet on the pattern.

3D Quail

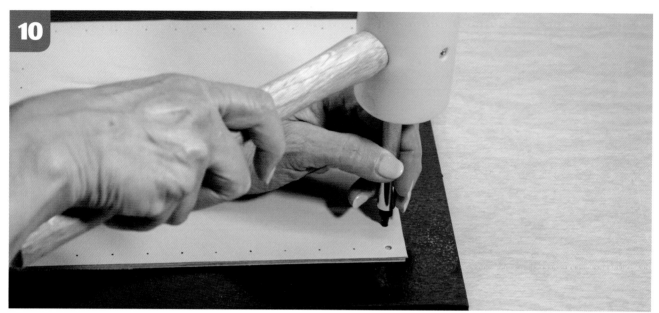

Punch the rivet holes. Use a leather hole punch for ⅛" (0.3cm) holes to punch through the leather where the dots are burned. Use a poundo board underneath to protect your tool and table. Pick out any leather that remains in the punched hole using a pointed tool such as an awl or heavy-duty needle.

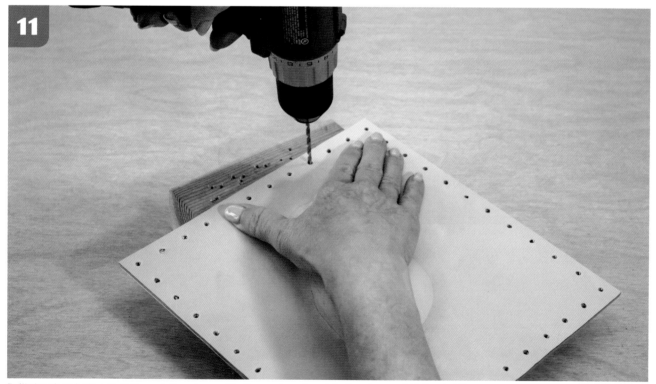

Drill the rivet holes. Drill through the plywood in the center of each hole using a ⅛" (0.3cm) drill bit and a piece of sacrificial wood under the project.

Tip:

Using a red pen helps you see where you traced. Check the transfer after a few minutes to see if the graphite paper is transferring onto the leather and not the back of the pattern.

Transfer the quail feet and log. Tape a piece of non-slip shelving liner to the table. Place your leather project on top of the non-slip liner. With the second quail pattern, line up the feet under the molded bird, using the tail as a guide. Tape the bottom of the pattern to the table in two places. Place the unwaxed graphite paper under the pattern, graphite side down, and trace the feet and log with a pen. Erase smudges and lighten extra dark graphite transfer lines with a kneaded eraser.

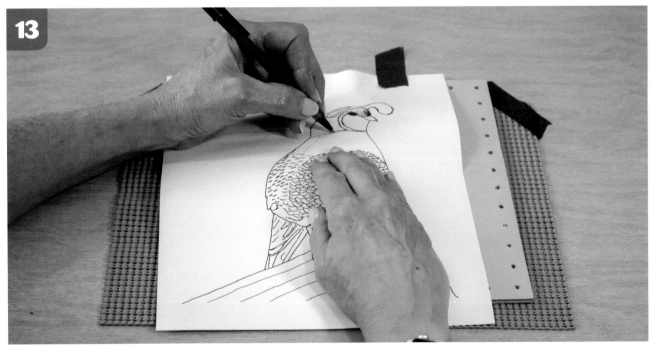

Transfer the quail head and body. To transfer the bird body and head, check the pattern against the molded bird. Sometimes the molding process can distort the original shape. For example, your molded bird may be slightly wider than the original pattern. If there is no major distortion between the pattern and the actual molded bird, line up the pattern over the bird. Tape the pattern in two places with painter's tape on the top edge and place the unwaxed graphite paper under the pattern, graphite side down. Start tracing the head and body of the bird pattern in the center. Hold the pattern in the center as you work your way down the sides. Do not press hard. Check to make sure the pattern is transferring onto the leather. When you are finished transferring the lines, erase smudges and lighten extra dark graphite transfer lines with a kneaded eraser. If there is major distortion between the pattern and the molded bird, however, you can either transfer the center of the pattern as described, and then mark the design on the sides of the leather with a soft pencil (2B or softer), or you can indicate the major design locations on the leather with a soft pencil by simply using the pattern as a visual reference.

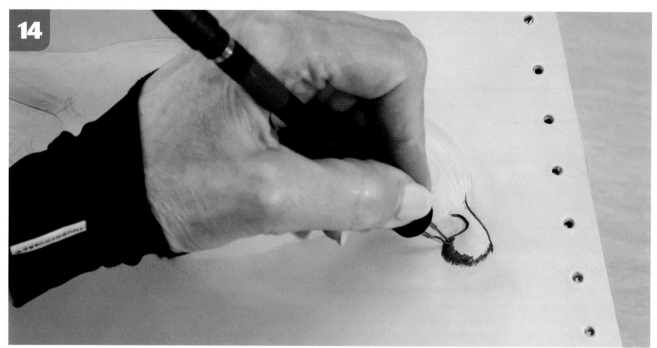

Burn the quail head: plume. Start burning the plume on top of the quail's head. Outline the plume with a small writer pen. I used a 0.8mm (1/32") ball writer. Whisk the lines off the end of the plume so they become thin at the ends of the lines, looking like little ends of the feathers. Fill in the rest of the plume by making parallel lines in the direction the plume bends, starting at the base on the head and continuing to the end of the plume.

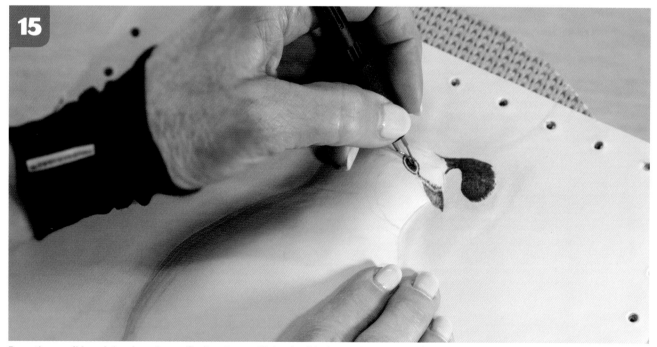

Burn the quail head: beak and eye. Outline the quail's beak with the small writer and fill in the beak with overlapping lines of different darkness to match the pattern. Next outline the eye, including the rim. Fill in the eye, except for the highlight, using the writer pen.

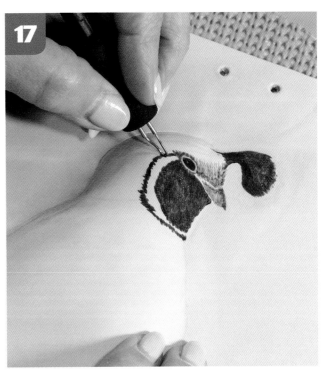

Burn the quail head: throat and face. Use the small writer to make lighter lines going from the beak upward toward the crown of the head, following the pattern. Use a medium writer to fill in the area under the beak to the white quail head markings. Use very dark overlapping lines in a slightly curved diagonal direction, mirroring the white marking curve. Start below the eye and move toward the outer lower edge of the dark area.

Burn the quail head: side. Use the same medium writer to make short, dashed parallel lines at the edge of the white head marking.

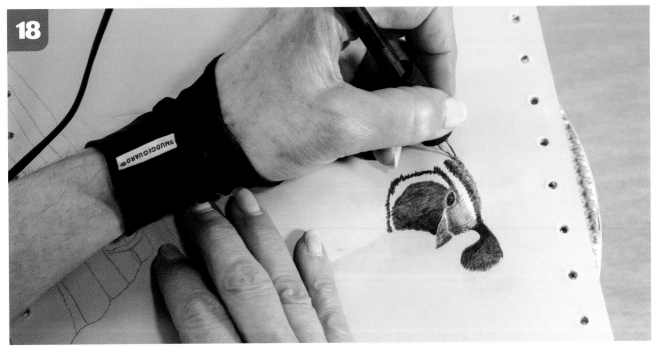

Burn the quail head: top. Use the same medium writer to make short, dashed parallel lines on the crown of the head. There is a darker row next to the white marking, and a medium color row between the dark row and the top of the head.

19

Burn the quail head: back. To create the dotted feather texture on the back of the quail's head, use your small writer to fill in this area with very light circular scribbling marks. Make a second pass with a medium tone burn of the circular scribbling. Note that you will have small circular texture on most of this area, but at the back and bottom, near the transition to the body, the circular texture becomes more oval in shape.

20

Burn the quail head: add texture. Add fine texture over the heavy dark areas (below the beak and on the plume) using a thin small or medium skew. Press very lightly to keep the marks thin and add texture with short marks in the direction you used to fill the areas earlier with the writer.

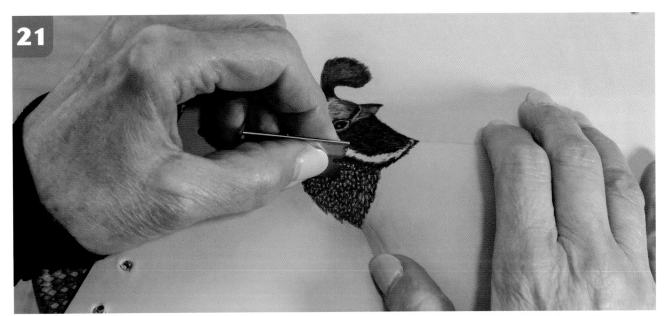

21

Burn the quail head: add highlights. Add a final layer of very dark circular and oval scribbling on the back of the head with the small writer pen. Use a razor blade to pick out the highlights of the circles and ovals to match the pattern.

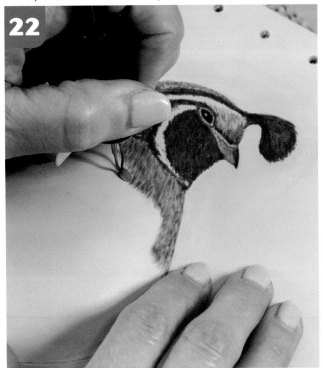

22

Burn the quail body: upper body. Using a small round-toe shader pen, fill in the upper quail body with a textured tone by tipping the pen into a more vertical position so the shading is created by the toe of the shader. In this position, move the shader back and forth in a short, vertical zigzag motion. Create overlapping rows to fill in this area. Use a thin round-heeled skew pen on lower heat to sparingly add detail texture over the area you shaded.

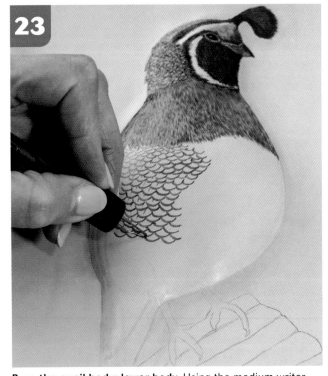

23

Burn the quail body: lower body. Using the medium writer pen, draw the feathers on the lower portion of the quail's body, following the pattern. The scalloped lines in one row intersect with the middle of the feather in the row above. A few of the feathers show a partial dark rachis (lines down the center of the feather).

3D Quail

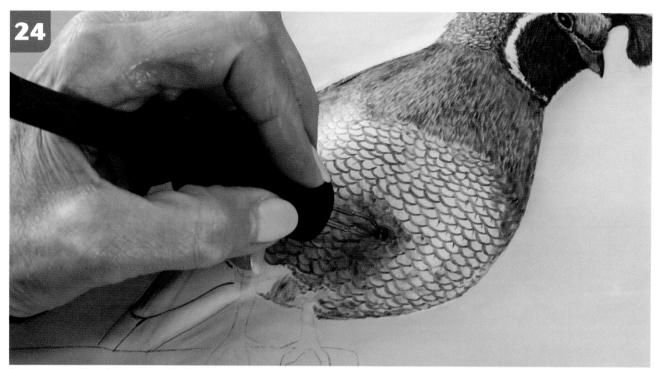

Shade the quail body: lower body. Using the small round-toe shader, add shading to the body feathers, following the pattern. Add light shading on the sides and upper center and darker shading in the center of the lower body, following the pattern.

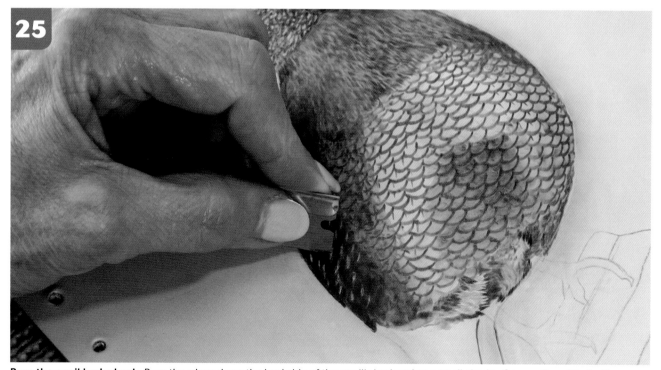

Burn the quail body: back. Burn the wings down the backside of the quail's body using a small shader. Scrape the white feather highlights on the wings, following the pattern.

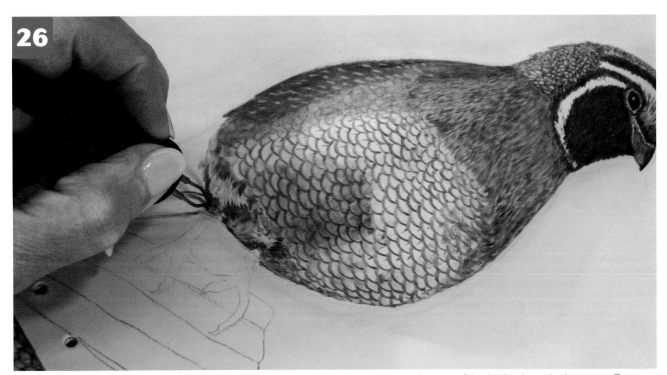

Burn the quail body: bottom. Use a small shader to burn the downy feathers at the bottom of the body where the legs start. To create the illusion that the white downy feathers are overlapping the dark area, burn the dark area first and pull dark streaks back into the white area with the toe of the shader.

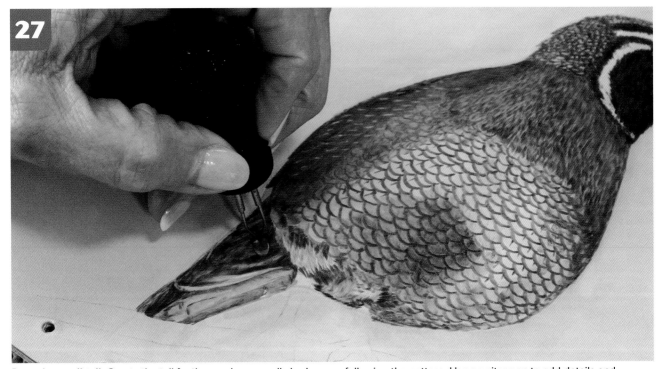

Burn the quail tail. Create the tail feathers using a small shader pen, following the pattern. Use a writer pen to add details and emphasize the contrast between the feathers.

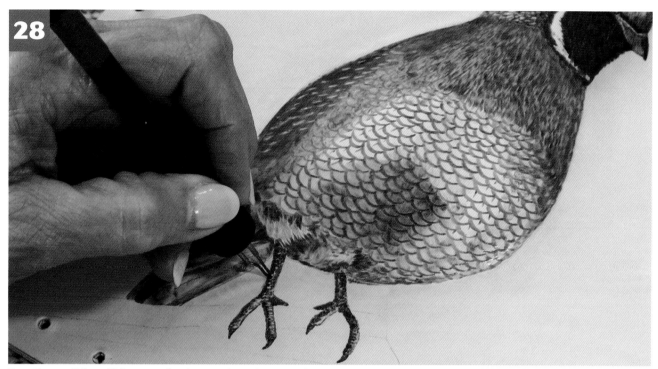

Burn the quail feet. Using a small writer pen, burn the quail's feet, following the pattern for the lines and shading.

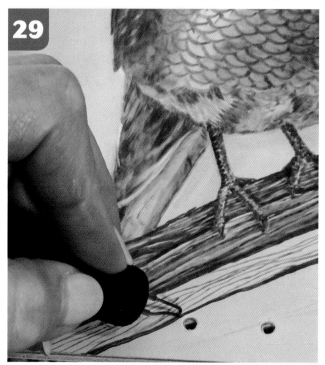

Burn the log: outlines. Using the medium writer pen, lightly mark where the log outline and dark streaks on the log will be. Erase the graphite lines. Next darken the major streaks down the log. Then lightly burn the wood grain lines between the dark streaks.

Burn the log: shading. Using the small round-toe shader pen, shade the log wood between the dark streaks, following the pattern. Shade in the direction that the wood grain lines are running.

Burn the log: finish. Using the round-heeled skew pen, emphasize the dark streaks and lightly add a few detail lines to the wood grain.

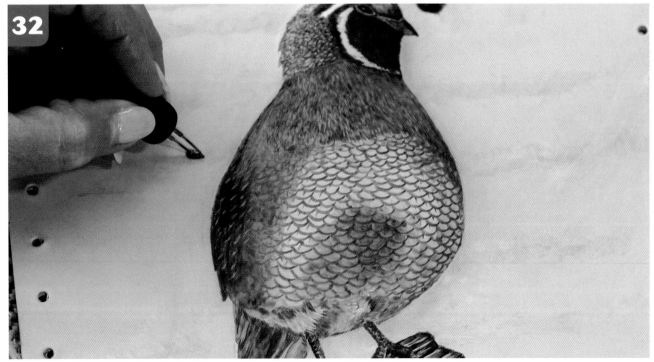

Burn the clouds. Create very light streaks of cloud in the background by using a circular motion with a flat shader pen. I used a transfer shader pen that looks look a miniature iron because the edges are slightly rounded and won't mark the leather. Test lightly burning clouds on a scrap piece of leather to get the right motion and burn color.

3D Quail

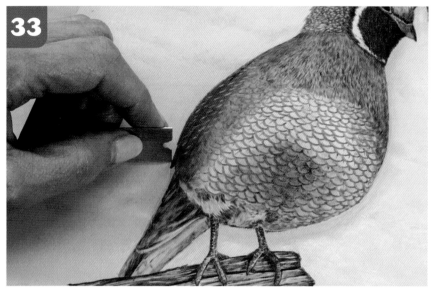

33

Clean up. Erase any remaining transfer lines. Use the edge of a razor blade to lightly scrape any edges that are bumpy and any dark splotches in the shading. See the section "Touching Up Mistakes" on page 47.

Tip:

If you want to add color to your project, add the color medium of your choice before you add the finish. You can choose from any of the color mediums in the "Adding Color to Pyrography" section on page 50. Test all the colors you are going to use on a scrap piece of leather. After testing the colors on your leather, test the effects of your finish over your color. For this project, I chose to leave the natural burning uncolored.

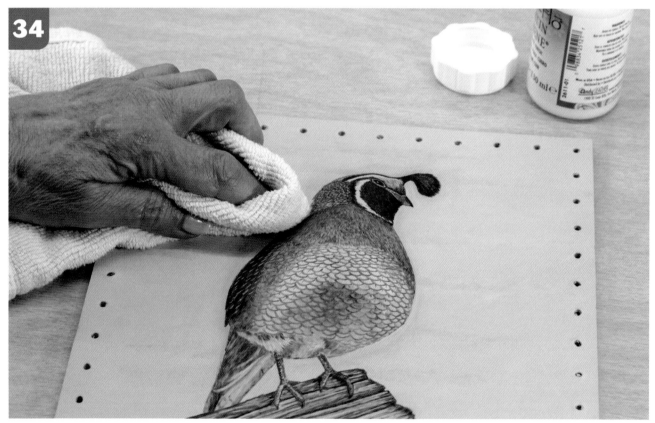

34

Add finish. There is no need to finish the edges of your leather because they will be hidden by the frame. Apply the finish to your project to protect the leather.

35

Add the rivets. After the finish is dry, add the rivets around the quail in the holes you created. To add the rivets, thread a rivet bottom, which has a long post, from the back of the plywood through to the top of the project leather. Snap a rivet cap onto the top of the rivet post. Place the rivet bottom onto the rivet setter base in the indentation designed to hold the rivet in place. Place the domed end of the rivet setter rod over the rivet cap to strike the rod with a leather mallet. I used a poundo board under the rivet setter base.

Tip:

If there is any wood or leather debris in the hole, the rivet post may have trouble pushing through. Use a small pointed modeling tool or awl to open the hole a little wider.

36

Add the frame. Place your project inside the rustic frame. Since my project is being mounted to the front, I used glue between the frame and plywood backing to hold the project in place.

Tip:

The rivet setter may leave a mark on the leather if you drive the rivet cap onto the rivet post too hard or at too much of an angle. If you do make a mark on the leather, use a clean, unheated shader tip to "iron" out the dent.

Chapter 6

PATTERNS

add back cover here

PLANNER

Steampunk Cover (Front Cover) - Enlarge 125% for actual size

add flap here →

Steampunk Cover (Back Cover) - Enlarge 125% for actual size

Steampunk Cover (Flap) - Enlarge 125% for actual size

Quail (Rivets) - Enlarge 300% for actual size

Running Horse (Rivets) - Enlarge 300% for actual size

Quail (Outline) - Actual size

LEATHER PYROGRAPHY

Quail (Shading) - Actual size

Running Horse (Outline) - Actual size

Running Horse (Shading) - Actual size

Woodland (Outline) - Enlarge 125% for actual size

LEATHER PYROGRAPHY

Woodland (Shading) - Enlarge 125% for actual size

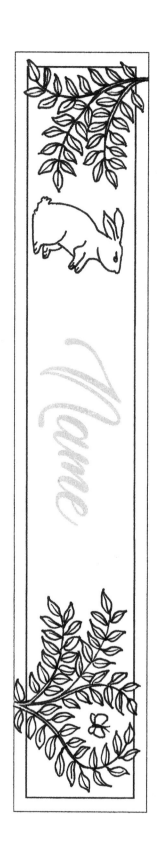

Bookmark, Coaster, and Key Fob (Outline) - Actual size

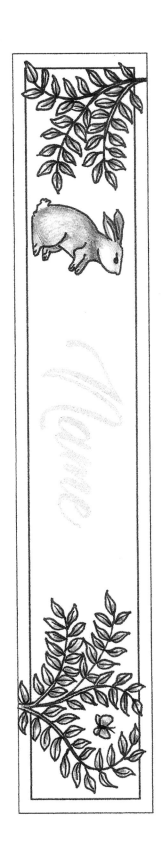

Bookmark, Coaster, and Key Fob (Shading) - Actual size

Celtic Borders and Celtic Mountain (Outline) - Actual size

Celtic Borders and Celtic Mountain (Shading) - Actual size

Celtic Tree and Celtic Wolf (Outline) - Enlarge 125% for actual size

Celtic Tree and Celtic Wolf (Shading) - Enlarge 125% for actual size

Patterns

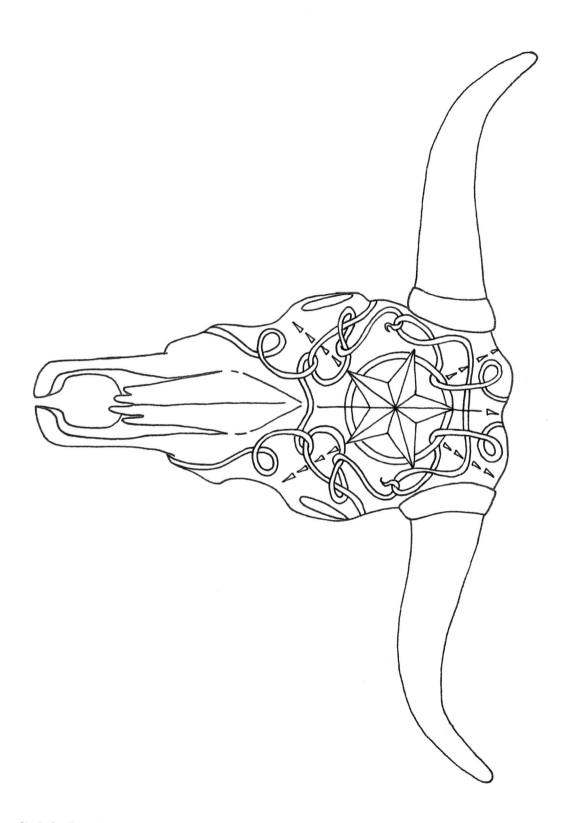

Longhorn Skull (Outline) - Enlarge 125% for actual size

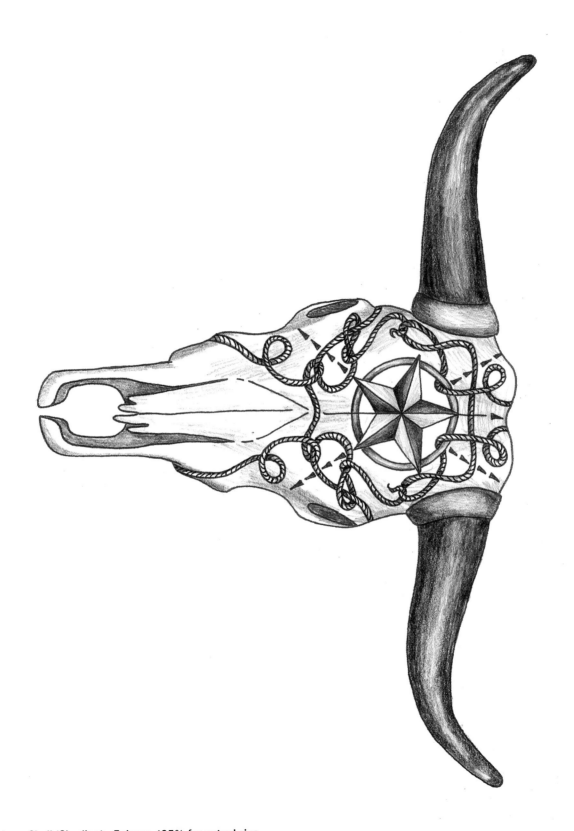

Longhorn Skull (Shading) - Enlarge 125% for actual size

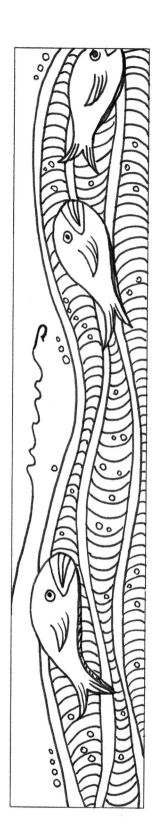
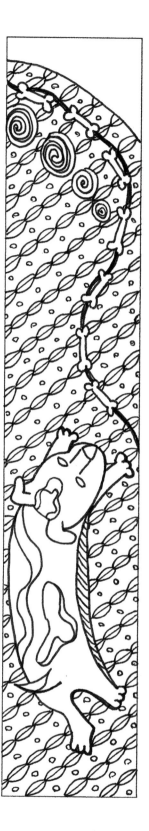

Zentangle® Bookmarks (Outline) - Actual size

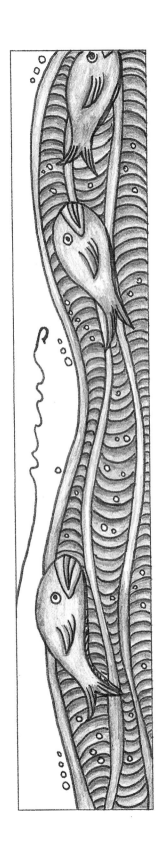
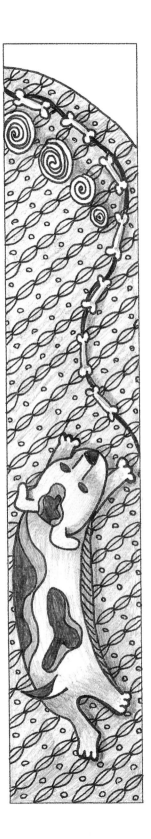

Zentangle® Bookmarks (Shading) - Actual size

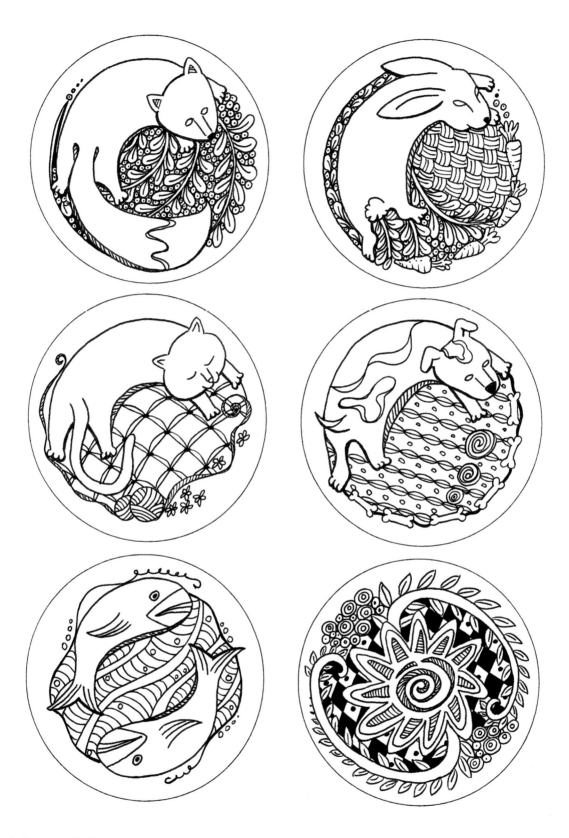

Zentangle Coasters (Outline) - Enlarge 125% for actual size

LEATHER PYROGRAPHY

Zentangle Coasters (Shading) - Enlarge 125% for actual size

RESOURCES

Leathercrafting Associations

International Federation of Leather Guilds
Summer: 3117 Babette Dr, Southport, IN 46227;
317-787-2586
Winter: 7318 Hwy 441 SE, Okeechobee, FL 34974;
863-467-8239
www.ifolg.net

International Internet Leathercrafters' Guild
president@iilg.net
www.iilg.org

Leathercrafting Museums, Shows, and Events

Museum of Leathercraft
Tandy Leather Museum & Gallery
1900 SE Loop 820, Fort Worth, TX 76140
www.tandyleather.com/en/museum-of-leathercraft.html

Southwest Leather Workers Trade Show
Prescott, AZ
www.leathercraftersjournal.com/
southwest-leather-trade-show

Rocky Mountain Leather Trade Show
Sheridan, WY
www.leathercraftersjournal.com/
rocky-mountain-leather-trade-show

World Leather Debut
Rhinelander, WI
www.leathercraftersjournal.com/world-leather-debut

International Federation of Leather Guilds Show
Columbus, OH
www.ifolg.net

Western Craftsmanship Symposium
Oklahoma City, OK
www.nationalcowboymuseum.org

Pendleton Leather Show
Pendleton, OR
www.pendletonleathershow.com

Leathercrafting Magazines, Newsletters, and Blogs

Leather Crafters and Saddlers Journal
315 Oneida Ave, Suite 104, Rhinelander, WI 54501
715-362-5393
www.leathercraftersjournal.com

Leatherworker.net Forum
www.leatherworker.net

Fine Leatherworking
1569 Solano Ave #625, Berkeley, CA 94707
415-800-2978
www.fineleatherworking.com

Leathercrafting and Pyrography Books

More Books by Fox Chapel Publishing

Fox Chapel Publishing Co., Inc.
903 Square Street, Mount Joy, PA 17552
800-457-9112
www.foxchapelpublishing.com

- Big Book of Pyrography Projects (Editors of Pyrography Magazine)
- Burning Night [DVD] (Sue Walters)
- Get Started in Leather Crafting (Tony and Kay Laier)
- Great Book of Woodburning (Lora S. Irish)
- Handmade Leather Bags & Accessories (Elean Ho)
- Landscape Pyrography Techniques & Projects (Lora S. Irish)
- Learn to Burn (Simon Easton)
- Leather Crafting Starter Book (Studio Tac Creative)
- Leathercraft (Linda Eastman)
- Little Book of Pyrography (Lora S. Irish)
- Pyrography Basics (Lora S. Irish)
- Pyrography Magazine
- Pyrography Patterns (Sue Walters)
- Pyrography Workbook (Sue Walters)
- Pyrography Workshop with Sue Walters [2-DVD Set] (Sue Walters)

- Sewing Leather Accessories (Editors of Skills Institute Press and Choly Knight)
- Stylish Leather Jewelry (Myléne Hillam)
- The Art & Craft of Pyrography (Lora S. Irish)
- Woodburning Project & Pattern Treasury (Deborah Pompano)
- Woodburning Realistic People (Jo Schwartz)
- Woodburning with Style (Simon Easton)
- Yearn to Burn: A Pyrography Master Class (Simon Easton)
- Fox Chapel Publishing also carries many pattern books; check out their website.

Pyrography Equipment Suppliers

Supplies from many of these manufacturers can be purchased at craft stores near you.

The Pyrography Store
Union Mills, NC
www.pyrographystore.com
Pyrography equipment, pens and tips, accessories, books

Razertip Industries, Inc.
301-9th Street North, PO Box 910, Martensville, Saskatchewan, Canada S0K 2T0
877-729-3787
www.razertip.com
Pyrography equipment, pens and tips, accessories, books

Colwood
44 Main St, Farmingdale, NJ 07727
732-938-5556
www.woodburning.com
Pyrography equipment, pens and tips, accessories, books

Walnut Hollow
1409 State Road 23, Dodgeville, WI 53533
800-395-5995
www.walnuthollow.com
Pyrography equipment, pens and tips, accessories,
wood products

Wall Lenk Corporation
1950 Dr. Martin Luther King Jr. Blvd, Kinston, NC
252-527-4186
www.wlenk.com
Pyrography equipment, pens and tips, torches

Mastercarver (and Burnmaster)
PO Box 574, Englewood, FL 34295
941-803-4972 or 888-877-8261
www.mastercarver.com
Pyrography equipment, pens and tips, accessories

PJL Enterprises (and Optima)
720 Perry Ave N, Browerville, MN 56438
320-594-2811
www.carvertools.com
Pyrography equipment, pens and tips, accessories, books

Leathercrafting Equipment and Leather Suppliers

Supplies from many of these manufacturers can be
purchased at craft stores near you.

Tandy Leather Factory, Inc.
1900 SE Loop 820, Fort Worth, TX 76140
877-LEATHER (1-877-532-8437)
www.tandyleather.com
Leather, stamping, dyes, finishes, supplies, accessories,
tools, project kits, tutorials, classes, books

Barry King Tools
1751 Terra Ave, Sheridan, WY 82801
307-672-5657
www.barrykingtools.com
Stamping, finishes, tools, books

Silver Creek Leather
Jeffersonville, IN
812-945-8520
www.realeather.com
Leather, stamping, dyes, finishes, supplies, accessories,
tools, project kits, books

Weaver Leathercraft
7540 CR 201, PO Box 68, Mt. Hope, OH 44660
800-430-6278
www.weaverleathersupply.com
Leather, stamping, dyes, finishes, supplies, accessories,
tools, project kits, tutorials, books

Goliger Leather Company
1580 Saratoga Ave Unit A, Ventura, CA 93003
888-44-HIDES or 800-423-2329
www.goligerleather.us
Leather, supplies

Hide & Leather House, Inc.
595 Monroe, PO Box 509, Napa, CA 94559
800-453-2847 or 707-255-6160
www.hidehouse.com
Leather, accessories, tools

Montana Leather Company
2015 1st Ave N, Billings, MT 59101
800-527-0227
www.montanaleather.com
Leather, stamping, dyes, finishes, supplies, accessories,
tools, books

Oregon Leather Company
110 NW 2nd Ave, Portland, OR 97209
800-634-8033 or 503-228-4105
www.oregonleatherco.com
Leather, stamping, dyes, finishes, supplies, accessories, tools, books

Panhandle Leather Company
4104 Amarillo Blvd West, Amarillo, TX 79106
806-373-0535 or 800-537-3945
www.panhandleleather.com
Leather, dyes, finishes, tools

Springfield Leather Company
1463 S Glenstone Ave, Springfield, MO 65804
800-668-8518
www.springfieldleather.com
Leather, stamping, dyes, finishes, supplies, accessories, tools, project kits, tutorials, books

Buckskin Leather Company
5220 1a St SE, Calgary, Alberta, Canada T2H1J1
888-723-0806
www.buckskinleather.com
Leather

Hermann Oak Leather
4050 North First St, St. Louis, MO 63147
800-325-7950 or 314-421-1173
www.hermannoakleather.com
Leather

Leather Wranglers
Albuquerque, NM
505-269-8563
www.leatherwranglers.com
Tools, books, tutorials

The Leather Guy
149 West Circle Dr, St. Charles, MN 55972
507-932-3795
www.theleatherguy.org
Leather, stamping, dyes, finishes, supplies, accessories, tools, project kits, tutorials, books

OA Leather Supply
PO Box 477, Wilkie, Saskatchewan, Canada S0K 4W0
306-480-4126
www.oaleathersupply.com
Leather, supplies, accessories, tools

Lonsdale Leather
76 West 6th Ave, Vancouver, British Columbia, Canada V5Y 1K1
604-873-6556
www.lonsdaleleather.com
Leather, dyes, finishes, supplies, tools

Miller Custom Leather & Tool Co.
Killeen, TX
www.etsy.com/shop/LeatherToolsByClay
Tools

Leather Stamps Tools by Sergey Neskromniy
Varna, Bulgaria
www.etsy.com/shop/LeatherStampsTools
Stamps

For additional supplier information, visit
www.FoxChapelPublishing.com/suppliers

About the Author

Michele Y. Parsons is an artist, instructor, and author deriving her inspiration from living in the shadows of the Blue Ridge Mountains in western North Carolina. She has been immersed in art and nature her entire life, spending her childhood  drawing, wandering in the woods, and exploring nature. Finding a way to combine these interests resulted in her gravitating toward creating art in wood—woodcarving and pyrography.

Michele earned a Bachelor of Fine Arts degree from Western Carolina University and minored in Biology. She apprenticed in traditional woodcarving for over six years with Paul Rolfe, and she studied under world-renowned woodcarving instructors such as Fred Cogelow, Rosalyn Daisey, and Desiree Hajny.

Michele worked for more than 30 years in Atlanta, GA, and Raleigh, NC, as a Graphic Designer, Art Director, and Director of Content Development for the healthcare education and IT training industries, which developed her understanding of teaching skills. She decided to leave the corporate world in 2010 to start her own business, **Parsons Wood Artistry**.

Since starting Parsons Wood Artistry, Michele has created and sold artwork for commissions and through galleries. In 2011, Michele participated in a historic international exhibition for pyrography at the Andrews Art Museum in Andrews, NC, which is believed to be the first museum exhibition dedicated to pyrography. Michele also demonstrates and teaches pyrography workshops across the US, most notably teaching yearly at the International Woodcarving Congress and Southeastern Woodcarving School. Gifted with an ability to teach others, she receives personal satisfaction when students learn pyrography and are excited about their newly found interest. To help students, especially in remote areas, Michele started selling pyrography equipment and accessories at discounted pricing.

Eventually she created on online store called **The Pyrography Store** (*www.pyrographystore.com*).

Michele has been an author for Fox Chapel Publishing since 2012, writing numerous articles in *Pyrography* magazine and contributing to *Woodcarving Illustrated* magazine, *Scroll Saw Woodworking & Crafts* magazine, and *The Big Book of Pyrography*. Through her experimentation with pyrography while writing for *Pyrography* magazine, she expanded the mediums she burned and found that she also loves burning on leather. She started offering leather pyrography classes, which led to the writing of this leather pyrography book.

Acknowledgments

I want to thank my best friend and husband, Tom Parsons, for his support and encouragement in my pyrography and woodcarving endeavors. He has given me the time, financial support, and advice to create my wood art business. I want to thank the Matt Tommey Mentoring program for helping me to recognize that God created me to be an artist and teacher, and for providing the tools to help me fulfill my purpose in life. I also want to thank several Fox Chapel Publishing employees that I have had the pleasure to work with over the past years—both in creating articles for *Pyrography* magazine and *The Big Book of Pyrography Projects*, various exposure in their woodcarving and scroll sawing magazines, and also in creating this book. I'd like to thank Mindy Kinsey for her many great years at Fox Chapel Publishing and for being wonderful to work with on projects; Bob Duncan for his help on reviewing the technical stability on projects and his ability to repair projects damaged in shipment; and Colleen Dorsey, Christopher Morrison, Katie Ocasio, David Fisk, and Mike Mihalo for their excellent, hard work on the book.

Index

Note: Page numbers in *italics* indicate projects (and patterns).

Photo Credits

The following images are credited to Shutterstock.com and their respective creators: leungchopan cover (leather background); Nor Gal pages 4–5 (leather background); yul38885 page 8 (leather rolls); Nor Gal pages 8, 11, 24, 50, 58, 116 (chapter opener tab).